# *Weathering the Storms of Life*

### *Navigating the Ship of our Lives*
### *Through the Stormiest Seas*

## Dr. Brandon S. Park

WEATHERING THE STORMS OF LIFE

PUBLISHED BY WAYSIDE BAPTIST CHURCH

7701 SW 98th Street

Miami, Florida 33156

ISBN 9781463561994

Copyright © 2011 by Brandon Park

Cover Design by GraceWay Media

Edited by Michelle Parker

Printed in the United States of America

2011 – First Edition

10  9  8  7  6  5  4  3  2  1

SPECIAL SALES

This book is available in special quantity discounts when purchased in bulk by corporations, organizations, and special interest groups. For information, please e-mail Karen@WaysideMiami.com.

# Contents

# CHAPTER ONE
## Weathering the Storms
*Preparing for the Inevitable*


Many years ago a blockbuster movie debuted entitled, *The Perfect Storm,* which was based on a true but unfortunate story. Back in October of 1991, Hurricane Grace collided with a cold front from Canada and a storm from the Great Lakes off the coast of Nova Scotia, creating what meteorologists have referred to as one of the worst storms in all of human history.

Hurricanes are much more powerful and dangerous at sea than they are over land. This particular ocean hurricane was so powerful that scientists said that the combined forces of U.S. and Russian nuclear arsenals could not contain enough power and energy to keep this storm system running for even a single day. Hurricane Grace had the highest waves measured in history – ten stories high with winds gusting at 120 miles per hour.

Meteorologists named Hurricane Grace, "the perfect storm." On October 27, a sword-fishing boat named the *Andrea Gail,* and its six-man crew, were headed home from Grand Banks, Canada with a hold full of fish. Although they tried to make it back before the storm crept into their path, in the middle of the night, the *Andrea Gail* found herself in the center of this fierce hurricane. "She's comin' on, boys, and she's comin' on strong,' radioed Captain Billy Tyne of the *Andrea Gail.* Soon after that transmission, Billy Tyne and his five crew mates disappeared without a trace. They were never seen or heard from again.

Maybe you have recently been hit by a storm. Not a literal hurricane, but a crisis of tragedy that blew into your life without warning, leaving you ravaged and riddled with problems. We all face storms in life. It has been said that only three kinds of people exist in this world: those who are going through a crisis, those who are coming out of a crisis, or those who are about to enter a crisis experience.

It doesn't matter who you are, no one has a life of all sunshine and no rain. Storms *will* happen! It is not a matter of if, but a matter of when. What are the difficulties that you have faced or currently are facing in your walk with the Lord? The Bible says in James that trials are given to test our faith and to make us more and more into the likeness of Jesus Christ.

Growing up as a kid in east Tennessee, I have distinct memories of coming home from school and turning on the television set to watch "The Dukes of Hazard." It was my favorite show. But one of the things that would always irritate me was those "tests" of the Emergency Broadcasting System that would interrupt my TV program. I hated those tests because they always seemed to come at just the wrong time, like right when Bo and Luke Duke were evading "Boss" Hogg in a high speed chase in *The General Lee*. There wasn't any advance warning that it was coming and there was no way to avoid it.

In the same way, the "tests" in life are a lot like that. They oftentimes come with no warning or announcement. They break in and interrupt our lives and we are left with the question, "Lord, why are you allowing this to happen to me?"

James 1:2 says, *"Consider it all joy, my brethren, when you encounter various trials, knowing that the testing of your faith produces endurance."* James tells us that we are to consider it pure joy when we encounter "various trials." The idea here of *various*, literally means in the Greek language, "multi-colored." We all know that tests and storms in life come in a variety of shades and colors. They may come in the color called physical. It could be a doctor with a bad prognosis about your health or a biopsy report. Tests can come in the shade of color called the "emotional." Perhaps it's a past event that you just can't seem to forget, a person you can't seem to forgive, or a state of depression you cannot seem to overcome. Trials can also color our lives in the area of finances, family problems, or marital difficulties.

So, we know that trials can come in a variety of colors and we simply cannot avoid them. The question we have to ask ourselves is how does God expect us to respond to those trials and periods of testing.

*My prayer for you is that through this study, you'll discover how to survive the sudden storms that come into your life and how you can grow in your Christian faith through your troubling circumstances.*

Two thousand years ago, there was another "perfect storm" in history. It was not perfect in its magnitude but it was perfect in its meaning. Jesus was going to teach his disciples the secret to sustaining and surviving these storms when they roll in unexpectedly. In Mark's gospel, we see a brief glimpse of how the Lord Jesus turned a storm into safety and a trial into a triumph. In Mark 4:35-41, the Bible says:

*"On that day, when evening came, He said to them, "Let us go over to the other side." Leaving the crowd, they took Him along with them in the boat, just as He was; and other boats were with Him. And there arose a fierce gale of wind, and the waves were breaking over the boat so much that the boat was already filling up. Jesus Himself was in the stern, asleep on the cushion; and they woke Him and said to Him, "Teacher, do you not care that we are perishing?" And He got up and rebuked the wind and said to the sea, "Hush, be still," and the wind died down and it became perfectly calm. And He said to them, "Why are you afraid?*

*How is it that you have no faith?" They became very much afraid and said to one another, "Who then is this, that even the wind and the sea obey Him?"*

It had been a wonderful day of ministry with Christ. Jesus had just fed five thousand people and the disciples were full of self-confidence and satisfaction. They were quite comfortable with the way circumstances were going. They were ecstatic and living on a spiritual high after watching how the Son of God just performed the impossible. At the end of the day, Jesus and His disciples, who happened to be seasoned sailors, decided to make their voyage to the other side of the Sea of Galilee.

Then, it happened. The wind began to rise. The clouds began to darken. The angry winds beat the sea and the water which was once on the outside of the boat was starting to find its way to the inside of the boat. The disciples, though they had plenty of experience with storms at sea, were scared out of their wits!

Are you in some type of a storm today and feel as if you are starting to take on water? If you're not, I'm happy for you—enjoy the ride! But take careful note of these principles because sooner or later you will find yourself in a squall. The question is, when you face the storms that bombard your life, how is it that you get safely to the other side?

# CHAPTER TWO

# Steering By Your Compass

*Remembering God's Promise*

Everyone knows the purpose of a compass in navigation. It's used to guide the traveler so that he may not be lost. No matter what position the compass is placed in – the needle always points north. Neither heat nor cold, summer nor winter, causes it to change. God's Word also never changes and when we choose to search our His promises for us, they serve as our source of "true north" and give guidance and direction for our lives.

Years ago, I attended a Pastor's Conference where Dr. James Merritt was teaching on this passage. He said in that sermon that when storms come upon us, there are three key thoughts we need to keep in mind: 1) Remember the Promise of Jesus, 2) Rest in the Presence of Jesus, and 3) Rely on the Power of Jesus. Those words have forever been ingrained into my memory and I reflect on them often whenever I face my own personal struggles. Those are the three guidelines that we can follow from this passage of Scripture when it comes to facing the storms of life.

If you notice in verse 35, Jesus said, *"Let us go over to the other side."* Jesus told them exactly what they were going to do. It was more than just a simple statement; it was a divine prophecy. Jesus Christ, being fully God and fully man, is omniscient, meaning He is all-knowing. He knew what they were going to face that day. If Jesus was capable of walking on water, don't you believe that He could also read and forecast the weather? He knew what was inevitable. But notice what He told those disciples – *"Let us go to the other side."* It was a command.

You need to realize that God's *commandments* are always His *enablements*. In other words, whatever God tells us to do as His followers, He will give us the grace and the ability to do it. Dr. Merritt also said, "If Jesus tells you that an elephant is about to lay an egg, don't just stand there gawking...get out the skillet!" So we see that when Jesus said to His disciples, *"Let us go over to the other side,"* there was nothing that was going to stop them from getting there. The Lord promised us in Isaiah 43:2, *"When you pass through the waters, I will be with you; and through the rivers, they will not overflow you. When you walk through the fire, you will not be scorched, nor will the flame burn you."* You see, the disciples could not drown because they were with Jesus.

Dr. Jerry Falwell, the Founder and Chancellor of my alma mater, Liberty University, once made a statement that I will never forget. He said, "You are immortal until Jesus' work is completed through you." If Satan could destroy your life, he would have done so a long time ago. He hates and despises anyone who is covered under the blood of Christ and would like nothing more than to see each and every one of us annihilated. Yet, God has a purpose and a plan for His people and therefore He makes a provision. He allows each of us the privilege of living every day until His work has been completed in and through us. When you face storms, you need to concentrate on the promises that God has revealed to you in His Word.

Whenever family came to visit, Grandma was usually found sitting in her favorite rocking chair reading her Bible. When her grown grandson and his wife came over for a visit, they noticed that Grandma continually talked about all the promises that Jesus had given to her in His Word. She was so full of Scripture that Bible verses seemed to flow effortlessly off of her lips. Yet tragically, on a routine visit to check in on his grandmother, this grandson walked into her home and realized she had passed away. Her body was found slouched in that familiar rocking chair, with her Bible open on her lap.

After the funeral was over, the young man told his wife, "I don't ever want that Bible to leave our family. Let's make it a family heirloom. In fact, why don't we follow in my Grandma's footsteps and read her Bible together as a family?" And so they did. However, one of the things that they kept noticing was that the letters "T & P" were hand-written in the margins across many of the pages of that well-worn Bible. They couldn't quite figure out what the letters "T&P" symbolized but they did notice that every time they came across those letters, they always corresponded to a promise in Scripture. They continued reading that Bible until they got to the very last verse in the book of Revelation in which she wrote: "All of God's promises to me are T & P. They are Tried and they are Proved!"

What a wonder, joy and blessing it is to know that every single one of God's 7,700 promises that are revealed to us in Scripture, His divine love letter to us, are "T & P"- they are tried and they are proved. Do you know what some of those promises are? Could you even name just a few of them?

I believe that one of the strongest reasons why so many believers today struggle under the burdens of life is because they are not diving deep into the pages of Scripture to see what it is that the Lord is trying to teach them. Isaiah 62:6 instructs us to "*Remind the Lord of His promises…*" Did you get that? When we find ourselves in the midst of difficulty, we are to remind the Lord of His promises to us! Does that mean that our Lord has a divine case of amnesia? Does God forget about what He told us? Of course not. He simply wants us to be searching His word to discover for ourselves what those promises are and to claim those promises by "reminding" them to Him in prayer.

Let me give you an example. When I first started pastoring, I was going through a difficult time during which I faced what many pastors experience on a regular basis -- *discouragement.* Our outreach programs weren't working as planned and our budget was down to the point that we didn't have the finances to pay the bills for that week. As if that weren't enough, I was also going to school as a full-time college student. I was discouraged, disheartened, and even tempted to give up. I kept on praying and asking the Lord to show me what to do next. I was giving it everything that I had and, quite honestly, I didn't know what else to do. But as I prayed, I sensed the Holy Spirit bring a verse of Scripture to my mind—a promise that I could "remind the Lord of." I claimed Galatians 6:9 which says, *"And let us not lose heart in doing good, for in due time we shall reap if we do not grow weary."* I felt as if that was my God-given promise. The Lord had reminded me that He had not called me to be *successful;* He had called me to be *faithful!* I was to be faithful in doing the work of the ministry and in His timing, He would provide the increase and we could then reap the blessings of God! In "due time," He certainly did. God's work done God's way will never lack God's supply!

When was the last time that you opened the pages of God's word, *outside of a church service?* One of the problems with Christians today is that they mark their Bibles, but they never allow their Bibles to mark them. Friend, when you come before God's word, you are not just coming to a book, you are coming before a Divine Person. What are you going to do with what this Person has told you?

When my wife and I were dating, we would write each other little "love notes" on a regular basis. I absolutely loved getting those.

Now that we're married, we still try to keep the romance alive by dropping a little note or card to one another every once in awhile. Just recently, she wrote me a heart-felt note letting me know how much she loves me and appreciates the things that I do for her and our family. Do you know what I do when I receive one of those "love letters"? I read it, and then I'll re-read it, and then I might set it aside for a while and then I'll go back and read it again! I just can't seem to put it down. I don't just throw her note in a drawer somewhere and forget about it. I cherish it and before long, I practically have it memorized! Why? Because I value, esteem, and regard what she has written to me.

God Himself has written you a love letter that we call the Bible. In it He has demonstrated His love for you by showing you His will, giving you His promises, and providing you with His comfort, just to name a few. It has well been said that "dusty Bibles produce dirty lives." But I also want to add that dusty Bibles also produce discouraged lives. Whenever you open the pages of God's word, you are encountering a personal and loving God. He wants you to crack open the pages of His "love letter" to you and allow His words to leap off of its pages and into your heart.

I admit it. One of the temptations that I as a Pastor tend to fall into is that I begin reading God's word not for what I can get out of it myself, but for that next sermon idea. The Lord is teaching me that when I read my Bible, I ought not to look for a message; I ought to look to meet Jesus. And when I meet Jesus – *I will become the message!*

In August of 2010, I went in to see my doctor because I had been struggling with my health for about a month. For the first few weeks, I thought nothing of it – only that it must have been a virus that my body would soon overcome. Yet when I never did get well, I knew that there must be something else wrong. When I saw my doctor, he ran a battery of tests, conducted a full physical examination, and asked me a myriad of questions. I could tell from the look on his face that he seemed very concerned. I finally raised enough courage to ask him, "Doc, what do you think is wrong?"

Then the bomb fell. He said, "Pastor Brandon, based on my physical examination of you, your spleen and liver are greatly enlarged. You have a lot of other symptoms that are causing me great concern. I am scheduling you for an immediate cat scan first time in the morning."

Now that he had my full attention, I pressed him further – "What do you think it could be?"

He replied, "I have to be honest with you. The reason I'm concerned is because you are exhibiting all of the classic signs of lymphoma – a cancer of your lymphatic system of which your spleen is the center."

For me that handful of words brought a crowded, thriving life to a screeching halt. I really did not expect to hear the "C" word – cancer. I was shell-shocked and numb the rest of the day. How would I tell my wife? What would be my prognosis? Come to find out – my questions led me to Google, which in turn resulted in more information than I ever wanted to know. It seemed I had every symptom and was at every risk for developing this specific type of cancer. You could imagine the lack of sleep I had that night. The following morning, I checked into the radiology department at my local hospital and waited to be called in. I brought my Bible with me and I distinctly remember praying, "God, if there has ever been a time when I needed a word from you – I really need it this morning. Please speak to my heart as only You can."

At that moment, I opened my Bible and randomly selected a psalm to read. I had never felt the Spirit of God speak to me so strongly through his word as I did that day in the radiology waiting room. I felt almost as if the Psalmist had penned those words for me at that moment in time. Psalm chapter 91 says:

*He who dwells in the shelter of the Most High*
*will abide in the shadow of the Almighty.*
*I will say to the LORD, "My refuge and my fortress,*
*my God, in whom I trust."*

*For he will deliver you from the snare of the fowler*
*and from the deadly pestilence.*
*He will cover you with his pinions,*
*and under his wings you will find refuge;*
*his faithfulness is a shield and buckler.*

*A thousand may fall at your side,*
*ten thousand at your right hand,*
*but it will not come near you.*

*Because you have made the LORD your dwelling place—*
*the Most High, who is my refuge—*
*no evil shall be allowed to befall you,*
*no plague come near your tent.*

*For he will command his angels concerning you*
*to guard you in all your ways.*
*On their hands they will bear you up,*
*lest you strike your foot against a stone.*
*You will tread on the lion and the adder;*
*the young lion and the serpent you will trample underfoot.*

*Because he holds fast to me in love, I will deliver him;*
*I will protect him, because he knows my name.*
*When he calls to me, I will answer him;*
*I will be with him in trouble;*
*I will rescue him and honor him.*
*With long life I will satisfy him*
*and show him my salvation."*

God used those comforting promises to speak directly to my heart and to renew my faith. Today, I am cancer free!

What problem are you dealing with right now? What difficulty are you experiencing? You need to "remind the Lord of His promises!" Dive deep into the pages of the Word of God and I can promise you that He will provide you with the comfort, provision, and direction that you need to weather the storm!

# CHAPTER THREE

# The Wind Behind Your Sails

*Resting in God's Presence*

In Mark 4:36-38, the Bible says, *"And leaving the multitude, they took Him along with them, just as He was, in the boat; and other boats were with Him. And there arose a fierce gale of wind, and the waves were breaking over the boat so much that the boat was already filling up. And He Himself was in the stern, asleep on the cushion; and they awoke Him and said to Him, "Teacher, do You not care that we are perishing?"* (emphasis mine)

Note that Mark was pointing out a detail that none of the other Gospel writers bothered to mention. He wanted the people to know that there were other boats out there on the sea that fateful night—but Jesus was in *his* boat. Did you know that if you are saved, the Lord Jesus will be there to guide you and He will be with you throughout your entire life? *He is onboard your boat!*

Now, the Scripture implies that this storm came upon them suddenly. The Sea of Galilee is like a bowl that is surrounded by mountain ranges. Rabbis used to say that God created Galilee just for Himself because it is one of the most beautiful bodies of water in all the world. However, it can also become a seething cauldron of severe weather. As cold air and warm air clash over the sea, storms can develop quickly and strike with little warning. In addition, the strong gusts of wind that cascade down the mountain ranges can produce some very dangerous waves.

Storms do have a tendency to come upon our lives suddenly and without warning. Just that one phone call from the doctor, a loved one, or your boss can send your life into a raging typhoon. But if you have the Lord Jesus in *your* boat, you can take comfort in knowing that you will not face it alone.

Many Christians have been raised to think that if things are going wrong in their lives then they are out of the will of God. But these disciples were not out of God's will. They weren't out there on the stormy Sea of Galilee out of disobedience, but out of obedience.

God uses problems to draw us closer to Himself and to enable us to sense His presence more strongly. Difficulties are sometimes our Lord's way of tugging at our heart strings to draw us closer to Him. I once heard a prayer that went something like this: *"Lord, I will go anywhere as long as You go with me. Lord, I will do anything as long as You do it through me. Lord, I will bear any burden as long as You bear it with me. Break all the ties to my heart except the tie that binds my heart to Yours."*

The Bible says in Psalm 34:18, *"The Lord is close to the brokenhearted; He rescues those who are crushed in spirit."* Joni Eareckson Tada (a godly Christian woman who is paralyzed from the waist down) said, "When life is rosy, we may slide by with knowing about Jesus, with imitating him and quoting him and speaking of him. But only in suffering will we truly *know* Jesus." That is so true because we will learn things about our relationship with Christ during storms that we would not learn any other way. They force us to become God-dependent rather than self-dependent.

I personally can testify to the fact that the most profound experiences that I have had in my walk with Christ have come out of a "valley experience." It was during those times that my heart was broken, that I felt abandoned or betrayed, or that I was experiencing that agonizing and heart-wrenching pain, that I discovered what it meant to know true intimacy in the presence of God.

Let me ask you a question: can you see farther in the day time or at night? You might think that the obvious answer to that question would be during the day simply because you could see miles away from a mountain top, or you could even see the sun that is shining upon earth 90 million miles away from our planet. However, it's only during the period of night, when our world is covered in complete darkness, that we have the uncanny ability to view stars that are shining billions of light years away!

What's the point? When you are walking through the darkest moments in your life experience, it may seem as if God is light years away. But if you would only look Heavenward by faith, you will soon find that the "Bright and Morning Star," Jesus, will soon be revealed most clearly. People may learn that Jesus is necessary while standing on the mountaintop, but it is during those times in the valley that they find that Jesus is all that they need. Paul testified to this fact in II Corinthians 4:17 where he recalls, *"We felt we were doomed to die and saw how powerless we were to help ourselves; but that was good, for then we put everything into the hands of God, who alone could save us."* (NLT).

Everyone knows that the words "test" and "school" are not mutually exclusive. When I was in seminary, I dreaded having to take those tedious exams in Greek class! But the same is true about life. We cannot go through this world without having periodic tests. The good news though is that God tests us on material that has already been covered in His class and His design is to graduate you on to the next level of spiritual maturity.

I have noted three different, yet positive, aspects about the tests that the Lord allows us to undergo. First of all, His tests are open book! You can use your Bible to consult the Author of wisdom. Secondly, you are allowed to cheat! We have the privilege of enlisting help and counsel from godly friends and spiritual leaders in the body of Christ. And thirdly, you cannot fail! Because even if you don't pass, God will continue to test you in this area of your life until you finally do ace His exam. Our Lord has a very peculiar way of teaching His followers in the school of life—first He gives the test, and then He gives the lesson. You may not completely comprehend His working in your life at the time, but don't worry. The lesson He is trying to teach you will eventually become apparent.

Look again at Mark 4. This is the only time in the Bible where Jesus is recorded as being asleep. I'm sure the disciples were wondering, "Lord, why are you at *peace* when we are going to *pieces*? Why are you at *rest* when we are so *restless*?"

Do you ever feel like that at times? Do you ever sense that your prayers seem to just bounce off the ceiling? I've got great news for you. God gives us a promise that He is always available to hear, to listen, and to respond. In Jeremiah 33:3 (which I have often heard referred to as "God's phone number"), He says, *"Call to Me, and I will answer you, and I will tell you great and mighty things, which you do not know."* The Lord Jesus gives us another promise of comfort and encouragement in Matthew 11:28: *"Come to Me, all who are weary and heavy-laden, and I will give you rest."*

The disciples had to learn an important lesson that day – there is no need to fear when Jesus is near. Jesus was present in the boat with them. Safety is not in the absence of problems, but in the presence of Jesus.

Often, we, as Christians, perceive God as being some kind of "absentee landowner" in that He saves us and then somehow gives us a gentle shove into the world and says, "Do the best you can!" Sometimes when we pray, we look up towards heaven and we say,

"God, do something *up there*. I am having a lot of difficulty *down here*."
Yet in John 14:16, Jesus said, *"He will give you another Comforter* [the Holy Spirit] *that He may abide with you forever."* If you have trusted Christ to be your personal Lord and Savior, Jesus has sent the Holy Spirit to take up residence in you. I Corinthians 6:19 says, *"Do you not know that your body is a temple of the Holy Spirit who is in you."* In the Old Testament, God had a temple for His people, but in the New Testament, He has a people for His temple. The Spirit of Almighty God is dwelling within you! That's why you need to learn how to "practice the presence of God." Here are just a few ways you can do that:

### Consciously think about His presence.

You need to stop several times a day and just get quiet before God. The Bible says, *"Be still and know that I am God."* (Psalm 46:10). Every morning, you ought to have a quiet time with God where you are able to look into His face and reflect upon His majesty.

In today's modern age, people are lonely. But you can be alone and not lonely if you will learn to practice the presence of God. These truths have changed the way that I go about my day-to-day life. I go for a drive with Jesus. I sit down and read a book with Jesus. I am consciously and consistently aware of His presence with me. You see, God has time for me as if there were no one else except me! And the good news is that He feels the same way about you. Do you feel lonely today? Remind yourself that God is present with you and thank Him for His presence.

### Carry on a constant conversation with God.

When you read the book of Psalms, you will find that the psalmist is talking *to* God, not *about* God. He's having a conversation with Him.

Pastor Brown once received a phone call from a woman in his church. She informed him of the fact that it seemed evident that her father, who was suffering from terminal cancer, did not have much time left to live. She asked if he could simply stop by and speak to her Dad as he had several spiritual questions he wanted to discuss. The pastor was happy to oblige and stopped by their house on his way home. As soon as he walked into the room where this man laid, it was obvious that the cancer had deteriorated and emaciated his fragile body. As soon as Pastor Brown walked in the door, the man blurted out a single question: "Why is it that I don't sense God? Has He given up on me?" Pastor Brown walked him through the story of salvation and he claimed that he was saved but he just could not overcome the feeling that God wasn't really interested in hearing his prayers and listening to the agony in his heart. He wanted to experience that closeness with Christ here on this earth in what little time he had left before meeting Him face-to-face. Pastor Brown stood and pulled a chair up close to his bedside and said, "Whenever you pray and talk to Jesus, I don't want you to pray as if He is some God who is far removed from you – because He is not. If you are a child of His as you claim, then His Holy Spirit is with you at all times. He will never leave you, nor forsake you. So whenever you begin to pray, I want you to imagine that Jesus Christ is sitting right here in this chair next to your bed. And whenever you read your Bible, I want you to imagine that it is Christ Himself who is reading the Scripture to you."

Several weeks went by and Pastor Brown received another phone call from this man's daughter. There was a solemn tone in her voice as she informed him that she found the body of her father that morning as she went in to serve him breakfast. But she said something to Pastor Brown that he would never forget. She said, "Pastor, ever since your visit, it was noticeably evident that my father was growing in his faith. He would talk about his 'Best Friend Jesus' and what He was teaching him in his word. He told me about what you shared with him – to pray and talk to Christ as if he were sitting in the empty chair next to his bed. Well, this morning, when I found my father – his body was still lying in his bed, but his head was resting on his folded arms on the seat of the chair next to him. He went to Heaven while praying in the presence of Jesus."

Learn to talk to God about anything and everything that is going on in your life and fellowship with Him just as you would your closest friend. Share with Him your fears and your frustrations; your joys and your sorrows. Have you ever heard someone say, "I pray, but my prayers never got above the light bulbs." That's part of their problem. They fail to realize that God is just as much below the light bulbs as He is above them. His divine presence is walking with you *down here*, so you don't have to feel like you must shoot your prayers into outer space. You talk *with* God, not pray *at* God. Learn to just converse with the Lord.

### Develop a spirit of praise.

The Bible says that *"God inhabits the praises of His people."* (Psalm 22:3) When you praise Him, God reveals Himself to you. Now remember, God is always present, but He manifests Himself to you when you praise. If you're having difficulty praying, just begin praising. As He fills you with His spirit, your problems will begin to fall into perspective. I can promise you, if you can get this truth riveted into your soul, it will change your life. God is near, and we can bask in the glory of His presence.

In many of the Native American Indian tribes, it was customary for boys to enter a rite of passage into manhood. The tribe would hold a special ceremony for the boy and the first action that he had to take in order to prove his manhood was for him to spend a night alone in a deserted forest and use his skills to find his way back home. The tribal leaders blindfolded the young man and led him to a dense part of the forest and told him to wait until he could no longer hear their footsteps before taking off the blindfold.

It was a very dark night on this particular evening—even the moon did not give a light glow on the land. And as the young Indian removed his blindfold, his surroundings were still so dark that it seemed as if he still had the covering over his eyes. He was terrified by the complete blindness. It was one night that seemed to last for an eternity. Every faint sound of snapping twigs or rustling brush caused his heart to race as his mind conjured up images of predators that lurked in those woods. As minutes turned to hours, the sun slowly peaked up over the horizon and the outline of the trees began to appear. For the first time, he was now beginning to make sense of his surroundings. As he looked around, he was utterly shocked to see the silhouette of a man standing over him with a bow and arrow... his father. Apparently, he had been there with him the entire night, watching over him and making sure that no harm would come his way.

One of the greatest benefits of being in God's family is knowing that when you feel lonely, you are never alone. Have you ever had anybody walk out on you? Have you ever had anybody leave you holding the bag? Have you ever experienced someone letting you take the blame? Have you ever had anybody leave you in the lurch? You see, a spouse can walk out on you, a child can run away from you, a business partner can betray you, and a close friend can abandon you; but, Jesus Christ will never leave you nor forsake you! I hope that you will always know that no matter how much darkness you may sense that you're in, you can have the confidence in knowing that your heavenly Father's presence is right there beside you. Death, distance, or darkness cannot hide you from the presence of Almighty God. He is right there watching you and waiting to guide you back home if only you will turn to him.

CHAPTER FOUR

# The Anchor in the Storm

*Relying on God's Power*

When you face your storms, you need to remember the promise of Jesus, rest in the presence of Jesus, and then rely on the power of Jesus. The Scripture says in the 39th verse of Mark 4, "*And being aroused, He rebuked the wind and said to the sea, 'Hush, be still.' And the wind died down and it became perfectly calm.*" The Bible says that the Lord rebuked the wind. This is the same Greek word that was used when He rebuked demons. But the Lord also calmed the sea and the verb that is used here literally means "to be muzzled," meaning that the sea was to be calmed instantaneously.

There were really two miracles that took place that day. There was not only the calming of the wind but also the calming of the waves. Everyone knows that long after a storm passes over water, the waves are still rolling. However, the Bible says that Jesus not only calmed the wind but instantly calmed the waves as well. It was truly an act of His divine power. Jesus did not keep the storm from striking the boat; He kept the storm from sinking the boat.

This story comes to a happy ending in Mark 5:1, "*And they came to the other side of the sea, into the country of the Gerasenes.*" The promise was fulfilled. The storm had passed. Safety and security were now a reality.

The "country of Gerasenes" was the area next to the Sea of Galilee where the town of Gerasa was located. This area was known as a land of rest and relaxation. Isn't it ironic that after they had battled this storm, the Lord leads them to a haven of rest? Our storms will pass too. Psalm 30:5 says, *"Weeping may endure for a night but joy cometh in the morning."* (KJV)

Jesus then asked his disciples, "Why are you so fearful?" In other words, "why did you doubt My power, My presence, and My ability to weather this storm with you?" I believe that is the same exact question our Lord asks of His children today when they neglect to rely on His power to bring them safely to the other side.

If we are to rely on God's power, there are two truths we should focus on from the passage. First of all, *fear looks at the storm*. Fear is what cuts the legs of faith right out from under it. II Timothy 1:7 says, *"But God has not given us a spirit of timidity, but of power and love and self discipline."*

Michael Pritchard said, "Fear is that little dark room where negatives are developed." Fear draws your attention away from what is good and onto your present circumstances. Fear never looks at the big picture but only at the seemingly magnanimous obstacle that is blocking its view of reality.

Peter demonstrated this for us in Matthew 14 when he saw the Lord walking on the water and desired to come to Him. The Lord gave Peter the miraculous ability to walk on those stormy waters, but then we see in Matthew 14:30 that Peter, in his state of fear, began to focus on the storm. *"But seeing the wind, he became afraid, and beginning to sink, he cried out saying, "Lord save me!"* Jesus responds by asking him the very same question he asked all of the disciples in our passage, *"O you of little faith, why did you doubt?"*

Nothing is so much to be feared as fear itself. When you honestly think about it, all the trouble that we experience is either a foe or a fear. But guess what? Our God is able to give you the power to face your foes and to fight your fears. When you are in trouble, you've got to get your eyes off of the storm, and off of yourself, and onto the Lord Jesus Christ.

The second truth is that although fear looks at the storm, *faith looks at the Savior.* Saint Augustine said that, "Faith is to believe what you do not see; the reward of this faith is to see what you believe." The greatest danger that day was not the storm but the disciples' doubt and lack of faith in their sovereign Protector. What happened to them was not happenstance. It was not a mistake. Remember, it was Jesus that sent them into that storm. It could be that God had engineered the entire thing. The Lord wanted His people to know that He was sufficient for them. He wanted them to look to Him in faith and to worship Him. You see, your storm is nothing but a superhighway to bring Jesus to you. It is the vehicle that moves you from a head-knowledge of Christ to the experiential understanding that God is who He says He is and that you can rely on His power to get you through. Andre Crouch has said, "For if I never had a problem, I would never know that God could solve them. And I would never know what faith in His Word could do."

Relying upon God's power means that you trust Him with every fiber of your being! Every relationship on planet earth is held together by trust. You put your money in the bank trusting that the bank will not go broke. When you go to the doctor you do so by trust—you trust that he knows the difference between a tonsillectomy and a hysterectomy (there's a big difference!) You go to the pharmacist by trust. The doctor gives you a piece of paper that looks like a dying chicken just scribbled some stuff down and you give that to the pharmacist and he starts mixing chemicals and says "Go home and take this three times a day." Friend, that takes a lot of faith and trust!

You get on an airplane and you trust that the plane is air worthy. You trust that the pilot knows the difference between north and south and that if you have a ticket going to Chicago, you don't find yourself in Cuba. All friendships are held together by trust. Your marriage to your spouse is held together by trust. We are even saved by the blood of Jesus Christ by trust.

You see, God has asked but one thing of man—that man should trust him. God has not asked man to understand Him because you and I don't have the intellectual capacity to do that. God has not asked man to explain Him. Our Lord said in Isaiah 55:8-9, *"For my thoughts are not your thoughts, neither are your ways my ways,' declares the LORD. 'As the heavens are higher than the earth, so are my ways higher than your ways and my thoughts than your thoughts.'"*

I grew up singing a great old hymn that says, "Trust and obey, for there's no other way to be happy in Jesus than to trust and obey." Are you trusting in the Lord's power to get you through your storm? Or is your soul rotting with the cancer of doubt and disbelief and you're looking at difficulties with a sour and cynical attitude.

The Apostle Paul knew that the secret to surviving the storm was to simply rely on the power of God. In 2 Timothy 4:14-17, Paul vents his frustrations of how many of his close companions had deserted him. Yet in the midst of that difficulty, he said, *"But the Lord stood with me and strengthened me"* (vs. 17). That word "strengthened" literally means, "to give power to." God's power in your life is at its best when you are at your worst. His power is at its greatest when you are at your weakest. When you feel as if you have hit rock bottom, you are in a position for God to take you to the top. God said to Paul, "I'm not going to take you away from the trouble you are facing, but I will be with you and strengthen you in that trouble."

God does not save us from the valley of the shadow of death. He does something far better. He walks with us through the valley of the shadow of death. Jesus Christ did not come to get us out of trouble; He came to get into trouble with us!

Many years ago Dr. Charles Stanley, a famous Christian author and televangelist, said that he was struggling with some opposition in his ministry. During that time an elderly woman from his church invited him to come to her retirement community for lunch. Although he was very busy and under serious pressure, he went and ate lunch with her. Afterwards she took him up to her apartment and showed him a picture hanging on her living room wall. It was a picture of Daniel in the lion's den. She said, "Young man, look at this picture and tell me what you see."

Dr. Stanley looked at the picture and then began to describe what he saw. All of the lions had their mouths closed, some were lying down, and Daniel was standing with his hands behind him. Stanley told the lady everything he knew to tell her as he observed that portrait. Then she asked, "Anything else?" He knew there must be, but he couldn't see anything else. She put her arm on his shoulder and said, "What I want you to see is that Daniel doesn't have his eyes on the lions, he has his eyes on the Lord." Like Daniel, our eyes should be steadfastly and confidently fixed upon Him during the good times and the bad.

Corrie Ten Boom knew where to look in times of trouble. She said, "When the train goes through a tunnel and the world suddenly gets dark, do you jump off the train? No! You have faith to trust that the engineer will get you safely to the other side. Hope remains that light is at the end of the tunnel."

Looking back at our passage, I know what you're thinking: "Why was Jesus asleep?" Quite honestly, I do not know but I can only speculate that perhaps the reason the Lord was asleep was because He had more faith in the disciples to steer the boat than they had in their Savior to calm the storm. I believe Jesus was aware of their circumstances the entire time but was waiting to see where they would put their faith and trust: in circumstances or in Him.

You can trust in God's power knowing that He has your best interests at heart. An unknown author expressed it this way:

*I asked for health that I might do greater things;*
*I was given infirmity that I might do better things.*
*I asked God for strength that I might achieve;*
*I was made weak that I might learn to obey.*
*I asked for riches that I might be happy,*
*I was given poverty that I might be wise.*
*I asked for power and the praise of men;*
*I was given weakness to sense my need of God.*
*I asked for all things that I might enjoy life;*
*I was given life that I might enjoy all things.*
*I got nothing I asked for but everything I hoped for;*
*In spite of myself, my prayers were answered –*
*I am among all men most richly blessed.*

We may ask amiss, but God always answers aright. Isn't it an awesome thought to know that the Lord is working through our circumstances to give us something far better than what we requested? The Bible says in Romans 8:28, *"And we know that God causes all things to work together for good to those who love God, to those who are called according to His purpose."* So when you face your storms, don't be disheartened, don't be discouraged, don't be dismayed. The storm ahead of you is never as great as the Power behind you. Simply rely on the power of God to get you through because He is more than able to sustain you, to protect you, and to bring you safely to the other side.

CHAPTER FIVE

# The Weather Forecast

*The Reason for Your Storms*

I am the type of person that asks the question, "Why?" to a lot of things about life. There are some things that I still just can't figure out. For instance:

- Why are there interstate highways in Hawaii?

- Why are there flotation devices under seats in airplanes and not parachutes?

- Why is the gas station 7/11 open 365 days a year, 7 days a week, 24 hours a day, and yet they still put locks on the door?

- Why can't the whole entire airplane be made out of that same material as that indestructible "black box"?

- Why is it that when I am driving, looking for directions, I have to turn the radio down?

- Why do they sterilize lethal injections?

- Why is abbreviation such a long word?

- Why do kamikaze pilots wear helmets?

And the last question that I have always had about life is why do they put locks on those gas station bathrooms? Are they afraid that somebody is going to break in and actually clean them?

I was amazed to hear that the average cost of rehabilitating a seal after the Exxon Valdez oil spill in Alaska was $80,000. At a special ceremony, two of these expensively saved animals were released back into the wild amid cheers and applause from onlookers. A minute later, they were both eaten by a killer whale. Have you ever had one of those days?

As a pastor, I am often called upon to be with a family in a time of crisis and the first question that is usually asked is, "Pastor, *why* did God let this happen?" That's a natural question because we need for things to make sense, especially in a time of loss. As one writer said, "we can bear the *what* of almost anything if we can just understand the *why*."

Unfortunately, the *why* of a particular problem or crisis is seldom ever discovered, and it may never be known. It is not our to ask why, for the why belongs to God. The question that we need to ask when we go through storms in life is the *how*. How are we going to respond to those circumstances God has placed us in that seem to make no sense?

We may never know the reason for a lot of the things that go on in life but God *does* want us to know the reason for why we have trials and storms in this world. The Bible is very clear as to why He places trials in our path. But why is it so important that you know the reason? The Bible says that if you cannot connect your experiences with Biblical facts, you will get discouraged and overwhelmed rather than "considering it all joy." That joy comes when you are in the very midst of your storm and you realize that God is up to something great within you. That realization is key to making it through. Sometimes the problem is not so much that we undergo trials, but that we undergo trials and simply don't know why.

One of my favorite comics to read is *Peanuts*. You can't help but love Charlie Brown. In one particular comic, Charlie is at the beach building a sand castle. He has worked tirelessly all day long building and sculpting to perfection that sand castle and it is absolutely perfect. Standing back to admire his project, he is quite proud of himself, until a wave rushes in and knocks the whole thing down. In the last frame of the comic, Charlie Brown stands there in disbelief and says, "There must be a lesson here, but I don't know what it is."

I believe that there are five major reasons why the Lord allows storms to pass through our lives. In the middle of your difficulty – there is a lesson, and it may be possible to know what it is.

First of all, it is to *test your testimony*. God gives you trials to test your faith. Christians are like tea bags; they aren't any good unless they go through a little hot water! Every Chrsitian wants to have a *testimony* without the *test*. And sometimes when God does give us the *test* all that we're left with is the *moanies!* When you go through hard times, God is putting your faith on the witness stand. Keep in mind that when God has allowed a storm to reach us He has a special and specific purpose in mind. (And may I remind you that He does block an awful lot! We won't know until heaven how often God has protected us from the junk that Satan has tried to throw at us!) Human nature is such that if we were never tested, few of us would have the motivation to pursue God no matter what the cost. He wants us to develop a strong faith, a faith that goes beyond our understanding and experience. In the school of life, God reveals His truth and promises to us, and then He puts us in the crucible so that we might learn that what we know in our heads and hearts is really true.

Did you know that there are some flowers that will not yield their perfume until they are bruised? Trials test our heart and they reveal what we are really made of. For many of us, we wouldn't know what areas of our life were weak if it weren't for trials. We wouldn't know the impurities that needed to be removed from our hearts if the fires of tribulation did not reveal them.

Do you want a good example of someone who had an appropriate view towards the storms that came into his life? Look at Job. He declared his hope in God by saying, *"Though He slay me, yet I will trust in Him"* (Job 13:15). That is the kind of faith and trust that we need to have. It is the kind of faith that says, "God, no matter what I am put through, I make a choice to stay faithful to You.

The second reason for trials is that they *increase our endurance*. James 1:3 says, *"Knowing that the testing of your faith produces endurance."* That word "endurance" is actually made up of two Greek words that mean "to remain under." In other words, we are to stay put in a trial until its purpose has been accomplished. The Bible says that we should not run *from* trials. Instead, we are to run *in* them. Rather than praying "Lord, *how* can I get out of this?" we ought to pray, "Lord, *what* can I get out of this?"

Many years ago, fishing for codfish up in the Northeast had become a lucrative business. The fishing industry recognized that a great market of codfish existed all over America, but they had a major problem in the distribution. At first, they simply froze the fish as they did all their other products, but for some reason, after the codfish was frozen, it lost its taste.

So the owners decided to ship the fish in huge tanks filled with fresh seawater. They thought for sure that would solve the problem and keep the fish fresh. But to their dismay, this process only made matters worse. Because the fish were inactive in the tank, they became soft and mushy, and once again lost their taste.

One day, somebody decided to put some catfish in the tank along with the codfish. Now catfish are the natural enemy of codfish, so as the tank traveled across the country, the codfish had to stay alert and active and be on the lookout for the catfish! Amazingly, when the tank arrived at its destination, the codfish were as fresh and tasty as they were in the Northeast.

Like that codfish, your adversity and the burdens that you bear could possibly be dropped in your path for a purpose. God will sometimes place those storms on you to challenge you, to strengthen you, to sharpen you, and to keep you fresh, alive, and growing.

Granted, at times, you may feel as if you have a great white shark in the tank rather than a catfish, but that adversity you are facing could very well be something that God is using to push you to be your best. It is the *struggle* that gives us the *strength*. Without some burdens and resistence, there is no potential for progress. Without the resistence of air, an eagle cannot soar. Without the resistance of water, a ship cannot float. Without the resistance of gravity, you and I couldn't walk. Just as kites rise against the wind, God wants you to know that the storm you are under could be a stepping stone to something better and to allow you to rise to new heights.

Trials also *teach us how to have real joy*. We tend to confuse happiness with real joy. Happiness comes from outside circumstances, but joy comes from within. Happiness meets surface needs, but joy meets your deepest needs. Happiness is like a cosmetic, but joy is like character. Happiness is like a thermometer, it registers conditions; but joy is like a thermostat, it regulates conditions. If I put my trust in happiness then I will be a victim of circumstances.

The Bible never commands us to rejoice in our circumstances but to rejoice in the Lord. Happiness works best when it is rooted in joy. Happiness is a wonderful thing but the Lord never commands us to be happy. The Bible says that we are to "rejoice in the Lord" and, since He never changes, 1st Thessalonians 5:16 says we are to "*rejoice forevermore.*" No matter what happens to me, I can choose to rejoice. The joy that we have in Jesus is steadfast in sorrow and it is triumphant in tribulation. Paul said, "I am exceedingly joyful in *all* my tribulations."

How can you tell if your source of true happiness is found in circumstances or in Christ? How can you tell if your joy is in your health? Take away your health; do you still have your joy? How can you tell if your joy is in your home? Take away your home; do you still have your joy? How can you tell if your joy is in your job? Take away your job; do you still have your joy?

One of the hymns that God's people have been singing for almost a century is "He Keeps Me Singing." This joy-filled song of praise begins, "There's within my heart a melody, Jesus whispers sweet and low." You can't sing this wonderful song without your heart being lifted.

But did you know that this song was born out of one of the strongest sorrows you could have ever imagined? The author of the words and the music of that song was a pastor and evangelist from Georgia named Luther Bridgers. He is said to have written "He Keeps Me Singing" after his wife and three sons died in a fire while he was away holding revival meetings in Kentucky.

The devil does not have a key that can unlock the treasury of your joy. Satan and circumstances cannot take away your joy. The only thing that can remove the "joy of the Lord" from your life is sin. That's why when David sinned against the Lord he prayed in Psalm 51:12, "*Restore unto me the joy of my salvation...*" You can only experience joy when it is rooted in and expressed through Christ. If you don't have the joy of the Lord, then your life is meaningless. To rejoice is a choice! Your attitude will determine your altitude. That choice begins with choosing Jesus. No Jesus, no joy. But when you know Jesus then you will know joy! The daughter of the great preacher, Dr. Adrian Rogers, wrote a poem about joy entitled, "*Joy Through My Teardrops.*"

*Joy through my teardrops and gains through my losses*
*Beauty for ashes and crowns from my crosses.*
*He binds up my wounds and he dries all my tears,*
*He calms every storm and He conquers my fears.*
*He gives me hind's feet to walk on high places.*
*He floods my soul with His heavenly graces.*
*When I am weak then His strength makes me strong.*
*I know I can trust Him, He has never been wrong.*
*Trials may come and temptations may avail me,*
*Though I may falter, He will never fail me.*
*So Satan, I bind you in His holy name.*
*For at the cross Jesus' blood overcame.*
*When the doubt comes, when I am lonely, when I am sad;*
*I will lift up my eyes to my Savior above, and Jesus will make me glad.*

Perhaps another one of God's goals for your trials is to *achieve your spiritual maturity.* God is more concerned with and committed to your spiritual growth than to your physical comfort. James 1:4, "*And let endurance have its perfect result, that you may be perfect and complete, lacking in nothing.*" God wants us to be made perfect which is another word for mature or Christ-like.

A master artist was sculpting some beautiful works of art out of stone as many bystanders stood there watching. His goal was to form a statue of a lion, and so he chipped and chiseled away until the image began to take shape. One of the onlookers watched in amazement and he asked the sculptor, "How in the world do you get that large piece of stone to look like a lion with just a hammer and a chisel?" The master sculptor replied, "I just keep chipping away anything that does not look like a lion!"

God does the same thing with us. The Lord's process of sanctification works just the same in us. He uses the hammer of hardship and the chisel of chastisement to chip away anything that does not look like Jesus Christ. His purpose is to sanctify us into Christ-likeness and to make us perfect or spiritually mature. God's goal is that we become conformed into the image of His Son. Oswald Chambers said, "If you are going to be used by God at all, he will take you through a multitude of experiences that are not meant for you at all; they are meant to make you useful in His hands."

A bar of steel worth $5.00 can be made into horseshoes worth $10. It can also be made into needles worth $350.00 or even delicate watch springs worth $250,000. What changes the worth of that same bar of steel? It is found in its being cut to a proper size, being blasted again and again in the furnace, hammered, beaten, pounded, finished, and polished. In short, it is the pain of the process.

Malachi 3:3 says, *"And He will sit as a refiner and purifier of silver, and He will purify the sons of Levi and refine them like gold and silver, so that they may present to the Lord offerings in righteousness."* Goldsmiths and silversmiths had an interesting way of purifying their gold and silver back in Biblical times. They would take the gold or silver ore from the mine and place it in an iron bucket attached to a long rod. Then, they would thrust this ore into a blazing hot furnace and, as the ore heated, the true gold or silver would sink to the bottom and the impurities of that ore would rise to the surface. The refiner would then remove the ore from the furnace, scrape off the impurities and plunge it back into the furnace. This process of purifying and cleansing this metal would be repeated over and over again.

Do you know when the gold or silver was finally removed from the furnace? Only when the refiner could look down into that gold or silver and see his reflection on the surface of that metal would he know that the ore was purified of all its impurities.

What do the fiery trials of life do? Our heavenly Refiner knows that they force us to bring all of our impurities to the surface so that He can gently remove them from our lives. Our Refiner has one purpose for placing us in the furnace. It is so that He can see His reflection in us. God wants to see the characteristics of Jesus emanating through your life. That is the reason for those fiery trials! Warren Wiersbe said, "When God permits His children to go through the furnace, He keeps His eye on the clock and His hand on the thermostat. His loving heart knows how much and how long."

Progress without pain is usually not possible. Let's be honest – most of the time, we are so caught up in our own plans and agendas that until there is a dynamic intervention that is strong enough and painful enough to get our attention, we really don't stop to take notice of what God wants to say to us.

We live in a skin-deep world. Gordon MacDonald gave this analogy. He tells a parable of a guy building a ship. And this guy was really into the ornate outriggings of ship-building. And so he built the most gorgeous sails you could ever imagine. He put teak wood on the deck of the ship. He installed all of the latest high-tech equipment for navigation. The ship contained all of the most beautiful furniture and the greatest paint job you could ever imagine.

But when it came time to put the weight in the keel that would stabilize the ship in a storm – this detail wasn't that important to him because nobody was going to see it anyway – so he sort of fudged on that aspect of the ship-building process.

Of course, on the first day he went out into the ocean, a storm came upon him and the ship capsized. This same guy who went out from the harbor with great applause came back with shame. Because, in Gordon MacDonald's words, he had "forgotten to build below the waterline."

One of the great tragedies of Christians today is that we're all caught up in the sails, and the wood, and the finer things of life – but our soul, which lies below the waterline is so hard for us to get at. Character and substance are shaped in the crucible of adversity. Show me someone who lives a carefree life, with no problems or trials or dark nights, and I'll show you a shallow person.

Finally, God uses trials *to bless through your brokenness.* Oftentimes, before God can use a man greatly, He must wound him deeply. Before you can bless, you must bleed. Before you can help, you must first hurt. When it seems as if the bottom of our lives has fallen out, it is then when God can fill us with the fullness of His presence. Brokenness produces blessedness. Oswald Chambers was right when he said, "If we are ever going to be made into wine, we will have to be crushed—you cannot drink grapes. Grapes become wine only when they have been squeezed."

There is a clear pattern in the Bible that teaches us that brokenness precedes greatness. Before Abraham became the father of many nations, he and Sarah were childless. Before Jacob could be blessed, he was wounded by an angel in a wrestling match. Before Joseph ruled Egypt, he was thrown into a pit, sold into slavery, and falsely imprisoned. Before Job's estate was doubled, he lost everything he had, including his family, his fortune, and his future. Before Moses became the great deliverer, he lost his position, his possessions, and his popularity. Before Joshua conquered the Promised Land, he went through the wilderness. Before Samson crushed the Philistines, he was blinded, binded, and grinded. Before David became king, he was renounced by his family, ridiculed by his foes, and rejected by his friends. Before Daniel could be used mightily, he had to spend the night in the lion's den. Before Hosea became a powerful spokesman for God, his wife betrayed him and returned to prostitution. Before Peter preached 3,000 souls into the kingdom, he denied his Savior three times and went out and wept bitterly. Before Paul brought the gospel to the Gentiles, he was blinded on the Damascus road.

Watchman Nee said, "Our spirit is released according to the degree of our brokenness. The one who has accepted the most discipline is the one who can best serve. The more one is broken, the more sensitive he is."

Oswald Chambers commented, "When God gets us alone through suffering, heartbreak, temptation, disappointment, sickness, or by thwarted desires, a broken friendship, or a new friendship—when He gets us absolutely alone, and we are totally speechless, unable to ask even one question, then He begins to teach us."

Sometimes God sees that our life is a mess and He breaks us so that He can remake us. If you sense that God is bringing you to a breaking point, respond to Him in humility. God gives you His attention when your spirit is broken, more so than when your spirit is proud. Psalms 51:17 teaches that, *"The sacrifices of God are a broken spirit: a broken and a contrite heart, O God, you will not despise."* It is a wonder what God can do with a broken heart, if He gets all the pieces.

One of the greatest promises in the Word of God and perhaps the most beloved verse of Scripture next to John 3:16 is the simple, yet profound promise in Romans 8:28 that I shared with you earlier. It says, *"And we know that God causes all things to work together for good to those who love God, to those who are called according to His purpose."* Things don't always turn out the way we want them to turn out. Things don't always happen the way we want them to happen. God doesn't always move in the way that we want Him to move. The principle that we need to ponder in this verse is that God always acts in our best interest. No matter what happens to you personally, God is going to use it for your good. And what is in your best interest? It is anything that makes you more like Jesus. Every single day, God is working in your life with one explicit goal in mind and that is to make you more and more into the likeness of His Son.

So what's the deal with suffering? Take a few moments to summarize and vitalize these truths into your heart by doing a simple Bible study. Here is a list I compiled on some of the many more purposes God may have in mind through your suffering:

## 1. An Opportunity through which We Get a Clearer View of God

Job 5:6, *"My ears had heard of you but now my eyes have seen you."*

## 2. A Tool God Uses to Make Us More like Christ

I Peter 4:1-2, *"Therefore, since Christ suffered in his body, arm yourselves also with the same attitude…"*

I Peter 2:21-23, *"To this you were called, because Christ suffered for you, leaving you an example that you should follow in his steps."*

### 3. An Instrument through which Our Life's Foundation is Exposed

Matthew 7:24-27, *"Therefore, everyone who hears these words of Mine and acts on them will be like a sensible man who built his house on the rock. The rain fell, the rivers rose, and the winds blew and pounded that house. Yet it didn't collapse, because its foundation was on the rock. But everyone who hears these words of Mine and doesn't act on them will be like a foolish man who built his house on the sand. The rain fell, the rivers rose, the winds blew and pounded that house, and it collapsed. And its collapse was great!"*

### 4. An Opportunity through which We Learn Humility

2 Corinthians 12:7, *"To keep me from becoming conceited because of these surpassingly great revelations, there was given me a thorn in my flesh, my messenger of Satan, to torment me."*

### 5. An Opportunity through which We Learn Obedience

Hebrews 5:8, *"Although he was a Son, he learned obedience from what he suffered."*

### 6. An Opportunity through which Our Faith is Revealed

1 Peter 1:6-7, *"In this you greatly rejoice, though now for a little while you may have had to suffer grief in all kinds of trials. These have come to you so that your faith—of greater worth than gold, which perishes even though refined by fire—may be proved genuine and may result in praise, glory, and honor when Jesus Christ is revealed."*

## 7. An Exercise Program through which Our Faith is Strengthened

James 1:2-4, *"Consider it pure joy, my brothers, whenever you face trials of many kinds, because you know that the testing of your faith develops perseverance. Perseverence must finish its work so that you may be mature and complete, not lacking in anything."*

## 8. A Means through which God Reveals Christ to Others through Me

2 Corinthians 4:7-11, *"But we have this treasure in jars of clay to show that this all-surpassing power is from God and not from us. We are hard pressed on every side, but not crushed; perplexed but not in despair; persecuted, but not abandoned; struck down but not destroyed. We always carry around in our body the death of Jesus, so that the life of Jesus may also be revealed in our body. For we who are alive are always being given over to death for Jesus' sake that his life may be revealed in our mortal body."*

## 9. A Means through which God Chastens Me for my Sin

Proverbs 3:11-12, *"My son, do not make light of the Lord's discipline, and do not lose heart when he rebukes you, because the Lord disciplines those he loves, and he punishes everyone he accepts as a son."*

**10. A Training Program through which You Become More Effective in Ministry for Him.**

2 Corinthians 1:3-5, "*Praise be to the God and Father of our Lord Jesus Christ, the Father of compassion and the God of all comfort, who comforts us in all our troubles, so that we can comfort those in any trouble with the comfort we ourselves have received from God. For just as the sufferings of Christ flow over into our lives, so also through Christ our comfort overflows.*"

# CHAPTER SIX

# Don't Go Down With the Ship

*How to Survive Discouragement*

The devil has a five-fold plan for your life:

*Doubt*—he wants to make you question God's Word and His goodness.

*Diversion* – he wants to make the wrong things seem so attractive that you will want them more than what God has in store for you.

*Defeat* –he wants to make you feel like a failure so that you won't even try.

*Delay* – he wants to make you put off doing something for God so that it never gets done.

*Discouragement* – he wants to make you look at your problems rather than at God.

William Ward said, "Discouragement is dissatisfaction with the past, distaste for the present, and distrust for the future. It is ingratitude for the blessings of yesterday, indifference to the opportunities of today, and insecurity regarding the strength of tomorrow. It is an unawareness of the presence of beauty, unconcern for the needs of our fellowman, and unbelief in the promises of old. It is impatience with time, immaturity of thought, and impoliteness to God."

We all understand what it is to live with discouragement because we have been discouraged before. It overwhelms us when we are overcome by certain expectations. We have expectations in virtually every area of our lives and when those expectations aren't met to our standards, we get disappointed.

A couple gets married and they have expectations about how their marriage should turn out. Yet time and again, after a few months or years, they come into a counselor's office and declare, "This is not the person that I married!" They had unmet expectations.

I have seen this happen to people in their careers. They change places of employment and, soon after, discover that their new job is not what they thought it was going to be. They quickly become discouraged.

Discouragement can even set in with God. We sometimes pray, "Lord, all these things are happening to me and I just don't get it."

Allow me to delineate four things that discouragement will do in your life:

**Discouragement will take a personal failure and transform it into a permanent deficiency.**

Maybe you used to be active in serving your church but then something happened. You saw it as a personal failure and you said to yourself, "I will never serve in the church again!" Perhaps somebody said something to you and it hurt your feelings. Discouragement prevents us from distinguishing the fact that just because something you did happened to fail doesn't mean that *you* are the failure. As a result of that "stinking thinking" you are forfeiting all the ways that God wants to use you in His service today.

English evangelist George Whitefield learned that it was more important to please God than to please men. Knowing that what he was doing was honoring to the Lord kept him from discouragement when he was falsely accused by his enemies. At one point in his ministry, Whitefield received a vicious letter accusing him of wrongdoing. His reply was brief and courteous: "I thank you heartily for your letter. As for what you and my other enemies are saying about me, I know worse things about myself than you will ever say about me. With love in Christ, George Whitefield." He didn't try to defend himself. He was much more concerned about pleasing the Lord.

**Discouragement will cause you to neglect your responsibilities.**

When we get discouraged, we neglect to do the things we were supposed to do. Our focus becomes diverted onto our real or perceived failures. The calling that God has placed on our lives becomes overshadowed by the myopia of our spiritual vision.

**Discouragement leads us to blame somebody else.**

Oddly enough, an elderly man, recently widowed and retired, decided to buy a motor home and travel. He had not bought a car in over twenty years. A sales representative proceeded to show him the various features of a particular RV. As he was explaining the features, the elderly man said, "What does this do?" The salesman replied, "That's the cruise control. You just get this big boy rolling down the highway, press that button, and it drives by itself."

The two men decided to take the RV for a test drive with the salesman behind the wheel explaining the features of the RV. The salesman said, "Sir, would you like to drive for a while?" The elderly man replied, "That would be nice." So, the two men pulled off the road and switched places.

All was going well and the salesman told the man that he was going to go to the back and stretch out on the couch. The salesman had just closed his eyes for a quick catnap when he heard a voice say, "What kind of mileage does this thing get?" The salesman looked up in horror to see the old man sitting in the chair beside him. He sputtered out, "Who...who's driving?" The old man said, "Oh, don't worry, I've got it on cruise control." The salesman dashed for the driver's seat, but it was too late. The RV went down an embankment, across a cornfield, and wrapped itself around a big oak tree.

In dismay, the salesman had the RV towed back to the dealership. When the two men got there, the owner of the dealership looked in horror to see this beautiful RV totally smashed. He said, "What in the world happened?" The old man replied, "The cruise control doesn't work."

There is a new epidemic in this world that we need to guard ourselves against. The name of it is "It's-not-my-fault-syndrome." Some people are plagued with this disease, and sadly they don't even know it! Many times, when it comes to finding the driving force of chaos in our lives, we need not look out the window, but in the mirror.

**Discouragement creates "myopia."**

I suffer from myopia physically. I have to wear high-powered glasses or contacts because I am not able to see clearly even a few inches away from my face. Discouragement does the same thing to us mentally and spiritually. You can't see anything but failure in your life. You can't see anything but failure anywhere you look. Have you ever asked somebody, "How are you doing?" and they say, "Oh, everything is horrible." You ask about their kids, their job, their health, their marriage and everything is bad.

The apostle Paul could have looked at his own life and said, "Everything is bad!" but he didn't do that. He wrote Philippians, a book that speaks of the indescribable joy that a believer in Christ has, while he was chained up in jail. The same guy who was in prison didn't let discouragement get the best of him. You don't have to allow discouagement to defeat your life.

The only survivor of a shipwreck was washed up on a small, uninhabited island. He prayed feverishly for God to rescue him, and every day he scanned the horizon for help, but none seemed forthcoming.

Exhausted, he eventually managed to build a little hut out of driftwood to protect himself from the elements and to store his few possessions. One day, after scavenging for food, he arrived home to find his little hut in flames, with smoke rolling up into the sky. The worst thing he could have ever possibly imagined had happened— everything was lost. He was stunned with disbelief, anger, and grief. "God, how could you do this to me!" he cried.

Early the next morning, he was awakened by the sound of a ship that was approaching the island. It had come to rescue him. The young man was shocked! He asked his rescuers, "How in the world did you know I was here?"

"We saw your smoke signal," they replied.

Do you feel like your "hut" is on fire? It's easy to get discouraged when things are going bad, but we shouldn't lose heart, because God is at work in our lives, even in the midst of pain and suffering. Remember that the next time you are tempted to get discouraged as you watch your little hut burning to the ground. It may just be the smoke signal that summons the grace of God.

My challenge to you is to simply not allow your burdens to sink your ship. Throw them overboard into the sea of God's grace and control of your life.

Growing up, I loved to go outside and play with my cocker spaniel named Galaxy. They say that dogs are man's best friend and I can certainly say that is true. I always had a blast playing outside with my dog. But Galaxy wasn't always the kind of dog that listened very well. When it was time to come home for supper, I would yell, "Galaxy, come!" But he more or less ignored me and continued to play in the puddles and chase after squirrels. I would continuously yell for him to come and follow me home but to no avail. Finally, I decided I was going to have to do something clever to get his attention. So I picked up a large branch and threw it in his direction. Galaxy thought I wanted to play "fetch," so he ran after the branch as fast as he could, picked it up in his mouth, brought it to me, and laid it at his master's feet. He had finally come home.

I wonder if the burden that you have today has not been given to you by God to cause you to come to His feet. Maybe He's tried to call you in other ways but you wouldn't come. What you are facing today may very well be the burden that God is using to bring you to His feet. Take whatever burden you may be facing and reframe that problem and readjust your perspective to think of them as vehicles that drive you to the heart of the Lord.

# CHAPTER SEVEN

# Rising from the Depths of Depression

*How to Overcome Despondency*

When the storms of life drag on for days, weeks, and even months, we begin to fall into a state of depression. I would equate depression to a storm that seems to have no sunshine in sight! But how does the Lord expect us to deal with how we feel? How are we to get up when we are down?

Years ago, there was a Midwestern lawyer who suffered from such deep depression that it was said that all his friends kept all knives and razor blades away from him in fear that he might commit suicide. This lawyer during his time of depression penned these words:

*"I am now the most miserable man living. Whether I shall ever be better, I cannot tell. I awfully forefode that I shall not...I what I feel were equally distributed to the whole human family, there would not be one cheerful face on earth. To remain as I am is impossible. I must die or be better."*

I find it interesting to know that the man who wrote these haunting words was none other than Abraham Lincoln.

John W. Stott, a great biblical expositor, once said "A Christian's two chief occupational hazards are depression and discouragement." I couldn't agree with him more! But what exactly is depression? Many psychologists have defined it as a feeling of helplessness and hopelessness that leads to sadness.

Here are some facts about depression that may surprise you:

- Depression is America's number one emotional disorder.

- Depression has become so pervasive in our society that it is now called "the common cold of mental illness."
- It is estimated that 35 million Americans suffer some degree of depression, and 10 million are severely depressed.
- One out of every eight people reading this book is in some state of depression
- 20% of the individuals in the average church are in a state of depression.
- The depression rates double with each new generation.
- Research shows that 1 out of every 7 people will get medical help for depression at some point in their lifetime.
- It costs over a billion and a half dollars a year to treat the depression of American people.
- 25,000 people will commit suicide this year and 15,000, or 60%, of those suicides will be directly due to depression symptoms.

Affluent America is known as the "depressive society". Recent research indicates that only 15-20 percent of Americans consider themselves happy. We do happy things and we have happy times but we are not happy people. We emit disappointment. "Life is not working out as we had hoped." The American dream has ripped us off in that it has not delivered the happiness it promised.

You may be thinking to yourself that, though your storms may be bad, you will never acknowledge the fact that you are in a state of depression. Christians are oftentimes taught that depression is some kind of evidence that they are living in a life of sin. However, I find it interesting to see how many of the godliest men in the Bible struggled with feelings of despondency. There is a *patriarch,* a *preacher,* and a *prophet* who each suffered from a state of such despondency, and they begged God to end their life!

Take Moses for example. Under the pressure of leading the Israelites through the wilderness, Moses was on the verge of a nervous breakdown. He was fed up with the whining and complaining of his people, and their criticism of his leadership. In Numbers 11:15, Moses prays, *"If this is how you are going to treat me, please go ahead and kill me – if I have found favor in your eyes – and do not let me face my own ruin."* Have you ever been so low down, discouraged, and depressed that you prayed, "Oh God, if you really loved me, you would have taken my life by now." Moses had reached an all-time low.

Queen Jezebel put a hit out on Elijah and all the prophets after they had won a great victory for God. Exhausted from running and feeling dejected by God, Elijah "went a day's journey into the wilderness. He came to a broom bush, sat down under it and prayed that he might die. 'I have had enough, LORD,' he said. 'Take my life; I am no better than my ancestors.'" (1 Kings 19:4)

When Jonah realized that God wasn't going to avenge his enemies, a people who commonly performed unspeakable horrors to neighboring peoples, he reached the point of depression where he prayed, *"Now, Lord, take away my life, for it is better for me to die than to live."* (Jonah 4:3)

All of these men were basically saying, "God, stop this crazy world! I want to get off! Let me die!" Moses had a *people* problem, Elijah had a *pity* problem, and Jonah had a *pouting* problem. Moses had his eyes on *others,* Elijah had his eyes on *himself,* and Jonah had his eyes on his *circumstances.*

These were good men. They loved God. They were successful. And if it could happen to them, if they could reach a breaking point to an extent where they desired nothing more than death itself, don't you think it, likewise, could happen to you?

Once a person falls into depression, the danger is that depression often degenerates into darker and darker phases. I think it would be helpful if we enumerated the phases of depression:

The Phases of Depression:

    1. A passive or listless feeling

    2. A prolonged period of sadness

    3. An attitude of "nothing seems to matter."

    4. A feeling of helplessness

    5. A feeling of hopelessness

    6. An attitude of feeling nothing is ever going to get better

    7. An idea that no one cares or understands

    8. A sense of rejection

    9. An emotion of "I would be better off dead."

    10. A desire for death itself.

You may have looked at that list and thought, "That's where I am!" If so, I am here to tell you that there is help for the helpless, and there is hope for the hopeless.

In the midst of a great depression, David wrote in Psalm 42:

1 *As the deer pants for streams of water,*
   *so my soul pants for you, my God.*
2 *My soul thirsts for God, for the living God.*
   *When can I go and meet with God?*
3 *My tears have been my food*
   *day and night,*
   *while people say to me all day long,*
   *"Where is your God?"*
4 *These things I remember*
   *as I pour out my soul:*
   *how I used to go to the house of God*
   *under the protection of the Mighty One[d]*
   *with shouts of joy and praise*
   *among the festive throng.*
5 *Why, my soul, are you downcast?*
   *Why so disturbed within me?*
   *Put your hope in God,*
   *for I will yet praise him,*
   *my Savior and my God.*
6 *My soul is downcast within me;*
   *therefore I will remember you*
   *from the land of the Jordan,*
   *the heights of Hermon—from Mount Mizar.*
7 *Deep calls to deep*
   *in the roar of your waterfalls;*
   *all your waves and breakers*
   *have swept over me.*
8 *By day the LORD directs his love,*

*at night his song is with me—*
*a prayer to the God of my life.*
*9 I say to God my Rock,*
*"Why have you forgotten me?*
*Why must I go about mourning,*
*oppressed by the enemy?"*
*10 My bones suffer mortal agony*
*as my foes taunt me,*
*saying to me all day long,*
*"Where is your God?"*
*11 Why, my soul, are you downcast?*
*Why so disturbed within me?*
*Put your hope in God,*
*for I will yet praise him,*
*my Savior and my God.*

This Scripture asks a question, "Why are you cast down, O my soul?" Why am I in a funk? To him it was a malady and a mystery. He was in depression but he didn't stay there. Here are two do's and one don't from the life of David on how to fight depression.

## Do Face the Fact of Depression

If you are depressed, don't deny it. Admit it. David admitted where he was. *"My tears have been my food day and night…" "My soul is downcast…"*

The symptoms of depression include:

-   Feelings of sadness, hopelessness

-   Insomnia, early awakening, difficulty getting up

- Thoughts of suicide and death
- Restlessness, irritability
- Low self esteem or guilt
- Eating disturbance - usually loss of appetite and weight
- Fatigue, weakness, decreased energy
- Diminished ability to think or concentrate
- Loss of interest and pleasure in activities once enjoyed
- Chronic pains that fail to respond to typical treatment

If you have 4 symptoms at the same time, this may be an indicator of major depression. If you have 3 symptoms at the same time, you may have chronic depression.

Some of greatest people who ever lived battled depression. Winston Churchill was, perhaps, the greatest Prime Minister in the history of Great Britain. He was famous for saying, "Never give up!" This same man called depression a "black dog" that followed him all of his life.

Somehow, we who are Christians find it hard to admit that we are depressed because we feel like depression is a sign that we are just not godly, that we aren't as close to God as we should be. In fact, some Christians teach openly that depression is sin. Nothing could be further from the truth.

Charles Spurgeon was one of the greatest preachers and one of the godliest men who ever lived. He said, "I, of all men, am perhaps the subject of the deepest depression at times...I am the subject of depression so fearful that I hope none of you ever get to such extremes of wretchedness as I go to...although my joy is greater than most men, my depression is such as few can have an idea of."

Have you found yourself where Spurgeon was? Are you there now? Tell the Lord, "Lord, I am depressed." Don't be afraid. He understands you better than you understand yourself. Illness begins with I. Wellness begins with WE. Healing begins with HE!

**Don't Fear the Force of Depression -**

Practically, all psychologists and psychiatrists agree that depression is caused by a combination of factors: sometimes physical, sometimes emotional, sometimes mental, and sometimes a combination of all three of them.

There are basically four types of depression:

1. *Endogenous depression*: chemical imbalance in the nervous system ...hormones out of whack

2. *Reactive depression*: a reaction to such things as the death of a loved one, or a severe personal setback such as divorce, breakup, loss of a job

3. *Toxic depression*: which would be caused by a viral illness, wrong type of drugs/prescription, or a poor die

4. *Psychotic depression*: This is the type that is linked to a "nervous breakdown," Over-exhaustion, a mental disorder, or brain disease.

Therapists say that the first two, Endogenous and Reactive, account for the majority of the cases of depression. They are the clinical causes of depression and I mention them because they coincide precisely with the Biblical causes of depression. Let's look at what caused people in the Bible to become depressed.

## Physical Weariness

*"My tears have been my food day and night, while people say to me all day long, "Where is your God?"* (Psalm 42:3)

David was saying, "I can't sleep!" He was not getting enough rest. He was mourning. Christians today are burning the candle at both ends, their nerves shot from the pressure of doing the job of four men. They are not exercising, not eating right, not healthy. It can happen to the modern-day workaholic and it can happen to stay-at-home mothers. But you can mark this down –

- when your body is physically rundown and worn out,
- when your diet is unhealthy,
- when you are not getting enough rest,
- and when your nerves are jangling from pressure and anxiety,

you are easy prey and a prime target for the monster of depression.

## Emotional Loneliness

In Psalm 42:5, David says, *"Why, my soul, are you downcast? Why so disturbed within me?"* Emotional loneliness often comes from upsetting circumstances. Maybe it's when we hear of the sudden death of a loved one. It could be that you have just gotten news that the tumor was diagnosed as malignant. Perhaps a spouse says after 25 years of marriage, "I don't love you anymore."

Immediately, our emotions come crashing down like a plane that has lost its engines. When this happens, so often what we want to do is withdraw into a shell and throw a pity party for ourselves. We need to keep in mind that depression is a relational problem; it doesn't just affect us.

There is a story of a New York police officer who saw a man standing on a bridge, apparently contemplating suicide. The officer climbed up the bridge, trying to talk him out of it. He said, "Look, before you jump, let me tell you why I think life is worth living, and then you tell me why you think life is not worthy living. Is that fair?" The man said, "I guess so." Well the story goes that after twenty minutes of talking, they both jumped into the water.

Emotional depression can be just as contagious as a physical illness. Your spouse or loved one who is depressed can make you feel depressed. You know, when things are rough, we sometimes tend to curl up into a fetal position and complain about how unfair life is. We sing that children's song:

*Nobody loves me, everybody hates me,*
*I think I'll eat some worms.*
*Great big slimy ones,*
*Little bitty tiny ones,*
*And oh, my, how they squirm.*

We lie down in a bed of self-pity and pull the covers of depression over our heads. So, even though depression is more than just a feeling, it does directly affect our feelings, and our feelings can bring on depression.

## Spiritual Guiltiness

*"I say to God my Rock, 'Why have you forgotten me? Why must I go about mourning, oppressed by the enemy?'"* (Psalm 42:9)

For David, his depression had maximized his foe and minimized his faith. Let me tell you something: The Devil is a master strategist; He is a great tactician. He knows exactly when and where to attack you and it is almost always when you are in a state of depression.

There is an old fable that says the Devil offered his tools for sale because he decided to go out of business. He displayed these tools: malice, hatred, jealousy, deceit, and several others. They each had prices marked on them. But one of them was set apart, marked with a much higher price than the others. When the Devil was asked why this particular tool was marked so high, he said, "Because that is my most useful tool. It is called depression, and with depression I can do anything with people that I want."

It doesn't matter how happy people around you seem to be, many are enveloped in the shroud of depression. For example, Christmas is "the most wonderful time of the year," according to the song playing on every radio station. People are bustling about buying gifts for those they love, decorating their home with cheerful decorations, and celebrating the season with parties and delicious food, the kind only made during this special holiday. In spite of all of the celebrating and seeming good cheer, Christmas has highest rate of suicides.

Sometimes, the reasons for our depression are circumstantial, beyond our control. Sometimes, we get down in the dumps that we have built with our own hands.

A man went to see a psychiatrist one time and he said, "Doc, I'm depressed." The doctor said, "Well how bad are you?" He said,

"Just terrible. I am so depressed I cannot even function. Doctor, you have just got to help me. What do you recommend?" The doctor said, "Well, normally I recommend that you take a trip." The man said, "I just got back from the Bahamas." The doctor said, "Well, why don't you go out and just buy a new car?" The man said, "I drive a BMW." The doctor said, "Well, maybe you ought to go out and build a brand new home." The man said, "I live in a $500,000 mansion."

The doctor said, "Let me get this straight. You just got back from the Bahamas, you drive a BMW, and you live in a $500,000 mansion." He said, "Why are you so depressed?" The man replied , "I make $100 a week."

Depression can be simply a result of our own sin and our own shortcomings. Our black cloud of depression is of our own making. Other times depression may be a spirit of heaviness that God spreads over His children to bring them to a point of realizing their sin, and repenting of it.

### Do Fight the Feeling of Depression

There is nothing wrong with getting depressed, but there is something wrong with staying depressed. Don't get me wrong; never tell someone who is depressed to just get over it. If they could, they would have done so a long time ago. That said, God has not called us to wallow in the valley of depression, but to walk on the mountaintop of victory. There is nothing that Satan likes better than to see a soldier of the Lord too depressed to fight a battle that has already been won.

Let me give you three simple biblical steps you need to take to battle depression:

## 1. Lie Down: You need Physical Refreshment.

Remember the examples of those three men from the Bible who all struggled with depression? Did God abandon them? Did He grant their wishes and wipe them off the face of the earth? Did they trudge through the remainder of their lives as hollow shells of the men they used to be? No, God provided exactly what they needed at just the right time.

Elijah was exhausted, running from the men who were trying to kill him. After he begged God to take his life, God, instead, gave him just the provision he needed. What did God do for Elijah? He let him sleep, gave him something to eat and drink, and then let him sleep some more. God gave him some much needed R&R. God the great Physician knows better than anyone how to take care of us. He knows that we have to eat right and rest well. He knows that if we are physically worn out other problems will surface.

The Bible teaches that it is a sin not to work. On the other hand, it is a sin to work all the time. We need to divert daily, withdraw weekly, and abandon annually in order to physically refresh ourselves. Vance Havner used to say, "We had better come apart or we will come apart." Not even Superman flies all the time. Martin Luther once said, "I have so much to do today I simply must go back to bed." Sometimes, that is the best thing we can do, just rest and get refreshment.

## 2. Launch out: You need Emotional Renewal

In Psalm 42:4, David says, *"These things I remember as I pour out my soul: how I used to go to the house of God under the protection of the Mighty One with shouts of joy and praise among the festive throng."* Even though

David is in a state of despondency, he still remembers what he did when he was not depressed – He was with the people of God worshipping the one true God.

Moses was stressed. He was a guy with way too many irons in the fire. Add to this the constant criticism toward him by the same people he risked everything for and led out of slavery. No wonder he wanted to pull his hair out.

According to Numbers 11, God gave him 70 elders to assist in the administrative duties that were burdening him. God told Moses that these 70 elders "will share the burden of the people with you so that you will not have to carry it alone." God helped him to see that he could not do everything. He taught Moses how to eliminate, delegate, and dedicate. The Lord brought others around Moses so that he would be emotionally renewed.

Many of us, like Moses, put too many irons in the fire, failing to realize that in due time we will get burned by that fire we've got our irons in. If you find yourself going through the blahs and the blues, put this book down and get out with the people of God and begin to serve. Find someone else who needs to be ministered to. It is amazing how your burden feels so much lighter when you pick up the burden of someone else. Proverbs 11:25 says, *"He who refreshes others will himself be refreshed."*

Dr. Carl Menninger, a famous psychologist, was once asked, "What should a person do if he finds himself in a state of depression?" Dr. Menninger's response was strikingly simple: "Lock the door behind you, go across the street, find someone who is in need, and do something to help them." There is someone out there that is hurting more than you are.

In Charles Colson's book, *Loving God*, he tells the story of an incredible ninety-one-year-old woman, known affectionately as Grandma Howell. As she moved into the twilight of her life, she had more than one reason to let depression take over, to just give up and die. Her youngest son had died. Her oldest son was in declining health. Many of her friends were dying and she had begun to believe that she had nothing left to live for.

One day, she prayed with all of her heart and told the Lord that if He didn't have anything more for her to do, she was ready to die. According to Grandma Howell, God spoke three words: Write to prisoners. After arguing with the Lord about her lack of education and her age, she wrote her first letter: "Dear Inmate, I am a grandmother who loves and cares for you, who are in a place you had not planned to be. My love and sympathy go out to you. I am willing to be a friend to you in correspondence. If you'd like to hear from me, write me. I will answer every letter you write. A Christian Friend, Grandmother Howell"

When the letter was sent to the Atlanta Penitentiary, the prison chaplain sent Grandma Howell the names of eight prison inmates. It was the beginning of an unbelievable ministry of encouragement. Over the next few months, this elderly woman carried on an extensive written ministry with hundreds of incarcerated men and women--- and all of it was done from her little room in a high-rise home for the aged in Columbus, Georgia.

According to Colson, writing to the prisoners was only half of Grandma Howell's joy. They wrote back! And their letters were warm, rich epistles of gratitude. One inmate who signed her name 'Grandmother Janice' wrote: "Dear Grandmother, I received your letter and it made me sad when you wrote that you think you may not be alive much longer. I thought I would wait and come to see you and then tell you all you have meant to me. But now I've changed my mind. I'm going to tell you now. You've given me all the love and concern and care that I've missed for years and my whole outlook on life has changed. You've made me realize that life is worth living and that it's not all bad. You claim it's all God's doing, but I think you deserve some credit. I didn't think I was capable of feeling love for anyone again, but I know I love you as my very own precious grandmother."

### 3. Look up: You Need Spiritual Revival

In Psalm 42:5, David says, "*Why, my soul, are you downcast? Why so disturbed within me? Put your hope in God, for I will yet praise him, my Savior and my God.*" David knew that if he was going to get out of this pit, He was going to need to look up and get his eyes off of himself. David shut down his little pity party. He got his chin up, his head up, and his eyes up, and he focused on the Lord.

Jonah needed a spiritual re-adjustment and revival in his life, as well. He had been sent to warn the people of Ninevah of their impending doom. These evil, murdering people were about to get what was coming to them, but, to Jonah's horror, they actually listened to him and repented. This was not how it was supposed to work. Jonah should have been watching God destroy Ninevah the same way he did with Sodom and Gomorrah. God was supposed to give him the satisfaction of watching them pay for their evil deeds. God had something else in mind to give to him. In Jonah chapter 4, God gave him what he so desperately needed, a new and fresh perspective.

God told Jonah that he needed to forget what He wanted, how he felt about the whole situation, and once again remember that God has the right to do whatever He so desires. God understood how Jonah felt, I'm sure, but he loved those lost people as much as he loved Jonah. Even as He was beginning His work in the hearts of the people of Ninevah, He continued to work in Jonah's, trying to teach him and grow him through this disappointment. I can't begin to tell you of the times when I was so depressed and, somewhere, God met me and His work in my heart was what I needed.

Elijah was depressed. Moses was depressed. Jonah was depressed. But each one came through, and you can too!

Years ago, a couple of adventurers tried to become the first to circle the globe in a hot air balloon. They took off from St. Louis, Missouri, rose to 24,000 feet, and started eastward across the Atlantic Ocean toward Africa. The prevailing winds carried the balloonists on a direct course for Libya, which was a big problem. Libya was ruled by a dictator who hated Americans and didn't want American balloons flying over his country. There was a pretty good chance that the balloon would be shot down if it crossed Libyan air space.

That brought up another big problem. Hot air balloons aren't easy to turn. In fact, they can't be turned at all. They're at the mercy of the wind. But, they can find different wind currents by changing altitude. At a higher or lower altitude, a balloonist can usually find a crosswind blowing in a different direction. So the quick-thinking adventurers started letting hot air out of their balloon and they dropped 6,000 feet. At that altitude, they found a wind that was blowing south, rather than east. Once they were safely south of Libya and its missiles, they heated up the balloon, rose almost 10,000 feet, and caught another wind that was blowing eastward toward their destination.

Balloonists are at the mercy of the wind and can only go in the direction the wind is blowing. Likewise, some people think they are at the mercy of circumstances. "Stuff happens," they say. "And there's nothing you can do about it." But, there is something you can do. Just as balloonists can change their *altitude*, you can change your *attitude*. And when you change your attitude, you change your direction. You are no longer at the mercy of circumstances.

David said in Psalm 121:1-2, "*I will lift up mine eyes to the hills— from whence comes my help? My help comes from the Lord, who made heaven and earth.*" The greatest medicine of all time for depression is God's love letter to you...the Bible. When you feel like your heart is about to break under the pressure of depression, remember Psalm 147:3: "He heals the brokenhearted and binds up their wounds." God wants to heal your broken heart, BUT first you have to give Him all the broken pieces. When you clothe yourself in the presence of God, God can heal and transform your life. There is no medication and no drug that can substitute for God, for his love, and strength. David gave the remedy for anyone who is fighting depression in Psalm 42:5, "HOPE IN GOD!"

Let me give you one final piece of advice. When you get depressed, remember God. Psalm 34:19 says, "*Many are the afflictions of the righteous, but the Lord delivers him out of them all.*"

Martin Luther often battled depression. During one particular time when he was passing through the deep depths of depression, his wife dressed in black and entered his study. He said, "Why are you dressed in black?" "I'm mourning," she said. "Why are you mourning?" he asked. She replied, "Because God is dead." Puzzled, Martin Luther declared, "Woman, that's nonsense. God is alive." She looked at Martin Luther and said, "If you believe that, then act like it and live like it."

If you do know Jesus, you can get up when you are down. The God that raised Jesus from the dead is the same God who can lift you out of the mire of depression and set your feet upon solid Rock.

# CHAPTER EIGHT

# When You Get Off Course

*How to Respond to the Problems of Life*

Do you think you're having a bad day? The following is a true story taken from a Florida newspaper:

A man was working on his motorcycle on his patio and his wife was in the house in the kitchen. The man was racing the engine on the motorcycle and somehow, the motorcycle slipped into gear. The man, still holding the handlebars, was dragged through a glass patio door and along with the motorcycle dumped onto the floor inside the house.

The wife, hearing the crash, ran into the dining room, and found her husband lying on the floor, cut and bleeding, the motorcycle lying next to him and the patio door shattered. The wife ran to the phone and summoned an ambulance. Because they lived on a fairly large hill, the wife went down the several flights of long steps to the street to direct the paramedics to her husband.

After the ambulance arrived and transported the husband to the hospital, the wife uprighted the motorcycle and pushed it outside. Seeing that gas had spilled on the floor, the wife obtained some papers towels, blotted up the gasoline, and threw the towels in the toilet.

The husband was treated at the hospital and was released to come home. After arriving home, he looked at the shattered patio door and the damage done to his motorcycle. He became despondent, went into the bathroom, sat on the toilet and smoked a cigarette. After finishing the cigarette, he flipped it between his legs into the toilet bowl while still seated.

The wife, who was in the kitchen, heard a loud explosion and her husband screaming. She ran into the bathroom and found her husband lying on the floor. His trousers had been blown away and he was suffering burns on the buttocks, the back of his legs and his groin. The wife again ran to the phone and called for an ambulance.

The same ambulance crew was dispatched and the wife met them at the street. The paramedics loaded the husband on the stretcher and began carrying him to the street. While they were going down the stairs to the street accompanied by the wife, one of the paramedics asked the wife how the husband had burned himself. She told them and the paramedics started laughing so hard, one of them tipped the stretcher and dumped the husband out. He fell down the remaining steps and broke his arm.

Now *that* is what I would call a bad day!

The fact of the matter is that you are going to have some problems in life and God is even going to orchestrate your circumstances so that you do have some problems. Trouble is a part of who we are. It is a part of our fallen human nature. No one ever gets beyond the reach of problems. There is no wall high enough, there is no door strong enough, and there is no man wise enough to escape all the problems this world has to offer. *Let me give you five ways that God uses problems in our lives*:

## 1. God Uses Problems to DIRECT ME

Here's a good principle to remember: *the problem that irritates you the most is the problem that God will assign to you to solve.* God uses problems to direct us. Sometimes it is those problematic irritations in life that reveal what we are passionate about changing.

God may sometimes place an obstacle in your path so that you do not miss the opportunities that He has to direct you. I think of the prophet Elijah after had had defeated the 450 prophets of Baal (1 Kings 19). After that incident, Elijah ran into conflict, he got depressed and he started to run away. He even got to the point where he asked God to kill him—he wanted his life to end. But God led Elijah by a brook for rest and refreshment. God supernaturally provided for Elijah by directing him to the brook, but then He did something else. He supernaturally caused the brook to dry up! That proved to be yet another problem for Elijah. What was God doing in all of this? Why did God allow the brook to dry up? It was because He wanted to move Elijah and redirect him towards His next plan for Elijah's life.

Another similar story is that of Jonah and the whale. God instructed Jonah to go to Ninevah and pronounce His judgment upon those people. Ninevah was east but Jonah decided to go west as far as he could and he ended up in the belly of a whale. That's a problem! But God allowed that problem to redirect Jonah into going where He intended him to go all along.

God may have allowed that problem that is in your life to redirect you. Perhaps you have been through a relational breakup. It hurts but God says, "I'm directing you…I'm drying up something in order to move you towards My choice for your life." It kind of reminds me of the song by the country group *Rascal Flatts* which speaks of how the breakups in the past lead us to the "one" we are to be with. The song says, "God blessed the broken road that led me straight to you."

Sometimes, we ask for a small blessing and get no answer – but find out later that God denied us because he wanted to give us something bigger. *You have to leave what you have before God can bring you to His best.*


## 2. God Uses Problems to INSPECT ME

How you respond to your problems speaks a lot about who you are as a person. God wants to see what's down in the well of our hearts because when the problems of life arise, it will come up in the bucket! You don't know how you will respond to a problem until you have the problem.

You see, your life is like a tea bag: when you go through a little bit of hot water, your true nature will come out. God told the Israelites when they were wandering around the wilderness for forty years that His purpose in keeping them in the problem was to find out their real nature. Deuteronomy 8:2 says, *"Remember that the Lord your God led you on the entire journey these 40 years in the wilderness, so that He might humble you and test you to know what was in your heart, whether or not you would keep His commands."* God said to the Israelites, "I brought you into the wilderness because I wanted to test you."

Any time there is a problem in your life, you can be sure that two things are going on – your faith is being tested by God and contested by Satan. Satan wants to discourage you, but God is testing your faith because he knows that faith is a muscle. Problems develop the muscle of faith. Problems let the world know what is really inside of you. That's why when you're in a problem, forget what you want and ask God what He wants you to have. God sends you into a problem, so you can find out who you really are.


## 3. God Uses Problems to CORRECT ME

Ken Whitten said, "Life is a school and problems are the curriculum." We learn more through suffering than we do from succeeding. God knows you will learn more through pain and problems than you do from prosperity. Sometimes those problems will reveal wrongful attitudes or motives in our heart. When we are faced with rules, there is something inside every one of us that says, "I'm not doing that." If we see a sign that says, "Wet Paint," what's the first thing you want to do? You want to touch the wet paint!

Mark Twain said, "A cat who sits on a hot stove will never sit on a hot stove again...and he will never sit on a cold stove either." Sometimes we have to get burnt in order to really learn the lesson God is trying to teach.

Ask yourself this question, "What is this problem teaching me? Is it showing a weakness? A blind spot? A character defect?

Remember, how you conduct yourself in the problem determines how long you stay in that problem.


## 4. God Uses Problems to PROTECT ME

**1 Peter 3:17** says, *"For it is better to suffer for doing good, if that should be God's will, than for doing evil."* Sometimes suffering is a blessing in disguise. Sometimes it is better to do what is right, but it is easier to do what is wrong.

The problems in your life may be God's ways of protecting you. If you don't believe that, go back to your 15 year class reunion and look at all those people you *could* have married! That will make you grateful for all those hard breakups!

Rick Warren told a story about how a businessman in his church came to him and said, "I have been asked in business to do something that is very unethical. If I do it, I will sin against God, but if I don't do it, I will lose my job." Rick told the man that if he wanted to do the right thing, he really had no other option biblically. He needed to take a stand for what was right.

The man didn't do what his company was asking of him and he was immediately fired. Two weeks later, he came to church carrying that morning's newspaper to show Rick Warren. The newspaper showed all of the top management of that company on the front page. They were all indicted for fraud and sent to prison. That man said, "Rick, if I had not done the right thing, that is where my picture would have been!"

God can use problems in life in order to protect us. The truth is we don't know about our tomorrows but God does. That is why there is no substitute for a consistent daily walk with God. Only when we get to heaven will we discover all the problems in life we avoided because we walked with Christ. We will never know on this side of eternity how God has protected us.

## 5. God Uses Problems to PERFECT ME

Here's another good *problem principle:* The success that you have in life will be determined by the problems you solve or create.

It was said of General Douglas MacArthur that the one thing that made him a great general was that he could see 50 problems and 50 solutions all at the same time.

What is God's ultimate goal for your life? It is to make you more like Christ. (Romans 8:28-29) God uses problems to knock off everything in your life that doesn't look like Christ. He keeps molding you and transforming you into the likeness of His Son, Jesus.

Pain and problems are a type of preparation like no other, allowing the unimportant to fall away and the critical to rise to the top.

As we move through this chapter, I want you to think about the biggest, most insurmountable problem you are facing in your life today. Here are five Biblical ways to resolve that problem:

**Visualize the Problem**

The passage of Scripture I want you to focus on is in 2 Chronicles 20. The King of Judah, Jehoshaphat, had a real problem. He had not one, not two, but THREE enemy armies that were plotting to overtake his nation and completely obliterate them. The lives of his family and God's people were in danger. And you thought you had stress in your life!

2 Chronicles 20:1 shows us that the first principle in overcoming the problems of life is to identify the enemy (visualize the problem). This is not as simple as it seems, unfortunately. A lot of people don't know who or what their enemy is. We often think that the enemy is a person who is trying to take something from us when our greatest enemy is actually ourselves and our own attitude. It is not so much the situation that gets us down but our response to the situation.

That brings us to another *problem principle:* How you see the problem could be the problem. Your perception of the problem will determine if you have the ability or the willingness to solve the problem. You've probably heard that old poem that says, "Two men looked out prison bars, one saw mud the other saw stars..." Your attitude makes all the difference.

You, and only you, have to take responsibility for your life. You control what you do. So why are you blaming someone else for where you are, how you are acting, and how you are responding? Winston Churchill said, "The price of greatness is responsibility."

You become responsible when you admit that your choices have consequences. When you look in the mirror and face that person squarely and say, "That person right there is the reason I am who I am, I am like I am, and I am where I am."

You are where you are today because of the decision you made yesterday and you're going to be tomorrow where you decide to go today. There is no such thing as indecision. People say all the time, "Well, I just can't make up my mind," but the fact of the matter is – they just did! You are always able to choose and to make a response.

If people are your problem and you have enemies, get up every morning with a smile on your face and you'll drive them straight up the wall. It's a wonderful way to live your life. Eleanor Roosevelt said, "No one can hurt you without your consent. They cannot take away your self-esteem if you do not give it to them."

Dr. Frankyl was a Jewish Physician who was captured by the Nazis during the Holocaust. His family was murdered in the gas chambers. His hair was cut off and all of his clothes and jewelry were taken. His name was replaced with a serial number, which was tattooed on his arm. He experienced horror and brutality while serving as a captive to the Nazi regime.

Yet one day, when he was naked and alone in a small single cell room, he became aware of what he later referred to as, "The

Greatest of Human Freedom." He had the freedom to decide how, in spite of this living hell, he would not let it control him. He decided not to be controlled by the Nazi's. He decided not to be controlled by the environment of hatred. Although he was in horrible conditions and painful circumstances, he made the decision that he would not be controlled by other people.

Now let me ask you a question: Are you allowing other people to control you - to control your life, your thoughts, or your emotions? If you are, you have crawled into a prison and handed them a key, and they are your warden. The Bible says in John 16:22, *"Let no man take your joy from you."* Remember, no one can hurt you without your consent!

**Verbalize Your Inadequacy**

Jehoshaphat was afraid because he was facing what seemed to be a hopeless situation. **2 Chronicles 20:12** says, *"We do not know what to do..."* There is only one kind of person that God does not help: the person who thinks he doesn't need any help.

Jehoshaphat goes on to tell God in that verse that even though he didn't know where to turn or what to do, *"... our eyes are upon you."* We need to get our eyes focused on the Lord. When it comes to our problems, too often we have our eyes on everything else except the One who can solve our problems. Obstacles are what we see when we take our eyes off of the goal. Someone has said: "Circumstances are like a mattress: if we're on top, we rest easy; but if we're underneath, we might suffocate."

We cannot live the Christian life on our own because we have a power shortage. **Zechariah 4:6** says, *"Not by might, nor by power, but by*

*My spirit says the Lord."* We need to allow the Spirit of God that resides within us to make contact with the external problems that are among us.

Several weeks ago from the time of this writing, I had a lot of problems and a lot of burdens weighing heavy upon me. There were a lot of deadlines and work that needed to be done regarding my responsibilities as a pastor. I'll never forget that night when I tried to go to sleep. The anxiety of knowing that I just didn't have enough hours in the day to accomplish all that needed to be done seemed to steal my joy. But that night I had one of those really weird dreams.

Let me just say parenthetically that I am not one of those preachers who believes that God audibly speaks to me in my dreams. But what I dreamt that night served to be an illustration of what God's Spirit wants to do inside of us in the midst of the pressure we are facing. That night, I had a dream that this immense burden was pressed up against my chest and I was having difficulty bearing the weight so much so that it felt as if I couldn't even draw air into my lungs. Then something happened. I dreamt that the Spirit of God breathed His life into me and literally "inflated me" in order to sustain me and handle the pressure. God did not take that burden away; He simply infused me with His strength and the ability to bear it up. I woke up that morning thinking to myself, *that is exactly what God wants to do inside of me. Rather than trying to handle this pressure on my own strength and on my own schedule, I need to verbalize my inadequacy and rely upon the inner strength of God's Spirit to get me through.*

Remember, **God will never allow more to be put ON you than he hasn't already put IN you.**

## Vitalize Your Prayer Life

So in the midst of this crisis, what did Jehoshaphat do? Verses 3 & 4 say that he proclaimed a fast and had all the people come together to seek the Lord. People came from every town in Judah to ask God for help and direction in knowing what to do.

The third principle for handling the problems of life is to take your problems to the Lord (to vitalize your prayer life). Prayer is oftentimes our last resort because we want to be able to work things out on our own. It's kind of like the deacon who came to his pastor one day and said, "Pastor, we've really got a problem and we can't solve the problem."

The Pastor said, "Well, I guess all we can do is pray."
The Deacon said, "Oh Pastor, has it really come to that?"

Prayer ought to be the *first* weapon that we use, not the last, when it comes to overcoming our problems. Jehoshaphat prayed, in effect, "God, I know you have helped me in the past. I know you can help me in the future. So please help me NOW!" I love what Ernie Merritt said, **"The problems that are over my head are under the feet of Jesus."** Tommy Tenney writes in his book, God Catchers, **"If your problems seem too big—perhaps your worship is too small."**

## Utilize Your Faith

Notice how God responded to Jehoshaphat's prayer in verse 15. It says, *"Do not be afraid or discouraged because of this vast army. For the battle is not yours, but God's."* You need to relax in faith! **Many Christians today are totally worn out because they are trying to**

**fight God's battles in their own strength.** God is trying to tell us, "Relax in faith and let Me work through you."

There was a time in my last pastorate when I had been diligently working for the Lord, but I was doing everything under my own power. And I was so tired. Finally I couldn't take it anymore. I said, "Lord, this stinks! I don't like it. I'm tired. I'm sick and tired. In fact, I'm sick and tired of being sick and tired." Then I said, "God, I give up!"

At that moment, I heard the Spirit of God speaking in that still small voice in my heart saying, "Brandon, that's Great! Now <u>I</u> can start working, because as long as you're out there trying to make your own plans and do it on your own, you're just going to mess things up. Relax and let me work through you."

Even though Jehoshaphat had 3 armies coming to war against him, twice in this passage God told Jehoshaphat not to be afraid (vs. 15 and vs. 17). Now, if you are one person and you see not one, but three military armies coming after you, if you have one ounce of insecurity it's going to come out right there! Yet God instructed Jehoshaphat on the need to relax in faith and allow God to fight his battles for him.

David said, *"Though war should rise against me, in God I am still confident."* So, quit whining about your problems. Quit whining about everything that's going wrong in your life. If you woke up this morning and didn't see your picture in the obituary column, square your shoulders, lift your hands and say, "I am more than a conqueror through Christ and I can do all things through Him who strengthens me!" REMEMBER: How you act in the problem determines how long God will keep you in the problem.

Verse 17 says, *"You will not have to fight this battle. Take up your positions; stand firm."* The reason why you don't have to be afraid of your problems is because God has promised to fight the battle FOR us and WITH us. Now what does it mean to "Stand firm" when you have a problem? It means to have a mental attitude of quiet confidence that says, "I'm going to trust God." God has recently been teaching me that it is never God's will for me to run from a difficult situation. Why? Because God wants to teach me that He is sufficient for any problem I may have in my life.

**Maximize Your Opportunities**

I found it interesting to discover that the Chinese symbol for the word "Crisis" is really two words combined into one. Crisis = problem + opportunity. How true that is! **Your problems are God's opportunities for Him to reveal Himself working directly in your life!"** *You can maximize the opportunities in the midst of your problems by doing these three things.*

**1. Move Forward in Action**

Verse 20 says, *"Early in the morning, they got up and left for the wilderness."* They didn't just sit on their laurels, wringing their hands and worrying about what would happen. They moved forward in faith!

Someone has well said, "The door to opportunity swings upon the hinges of opposition." I believe that sometimes God wants us to push through that door! You see, Christianity is an action faith – God wants you to be proactive and take charge as you walk in dependence through the power of His Spirit. Don't think that you can solve your problems on your own strength…but understand this: **God gave you two ends with which to solve your problems: A head with which to think and a derriere to sit on and do nothing – heads we win and tails we lose!** When it comes to your problems, the worst thing you can do is NOTHING! God can only steer you in finding a solution to your problem when you get moving. He has placed the initiative within you and He has given you abundant resources, as He has placed within the Word of God every principle needed to solve every problem you encounter.

### 2. Move Forward in Obedience

The second part of verse 20 says, *"Have faith in the LORD your God and you will be upheld; have faith in his prophets [the Word of God] and you will be successful."*

A long haired boy once asked his Dad if he would buy him a car. The Dad said, "If you keep your grades up, read your Bible every day, and cut your long hair, I'll consider it."

Six weeks passed and the boy came to the Dad and said, "Here is my report card, I got straight A's and I've been reading my Bible twice a day every day."

The Father said, "Yes, but your hair is still long."

The Son said, "Yes, but I've been reading the Bible and Jesus and His 12 disciples had long hair."

The Father said, "Well, if you've been reading your Bible, you would also know that Jesus and His 12 disciples *walked* everywhere they went."

Here's the point: **If you want what the Father has, you have to do what the Father wants.** Someone once said that the word B.I.B.L.E. stands for Basic Instructions Before Leaving Earth! You must not only read it, but do it.

Why do we come to God for knowledge and wisdom in seeking His will when we're not living in obedience to what He has already revealed in His will? God is saying, "Why should I reveal my will to you in this area of your life if you continue to refuse to obey me in these other areas of your life?" Maybe you're having financial problems. God has already told you in His Word, "I want you to tithe." But you say, "I'm not going to tithe! That's too much money!" God says, "All right, you're not going to tithe. I'll let you stay in debt." By the way, do you know what the acronym is for D.E.B.T. is? **Doing Everything But Tithing.** Don't ask for God's blessing in helping you get out of debt until you tithe.

People today are doing all kinds of things in order to satisfy their greeds through material possessions. They refuse to do any less than to have the nicest cars, houses and designer clothes. Yet they come before God in prayer and say, "Lord, why am I having all of these financial problems? Doesn't the Bible say, *'My God shall supply all your needs according to His riches in glory by Christ Jesus?'*" Yes, but God says, **"I will supply all your *needs* but not all your *greeds.*"**

Maybe your problem is concerning your marriage relationship. God may say to the husband, "You've been a little mouthy with your wife lately. You need to go and apologize to her." The Word of God teaches that He will not hear our prayers if we are at odds with our spouse. It's sort of like that old German Proverb that says, "If at first you don't succeed, try doing it like your wife told you to in the first place."

## 3. Move Forward in Anticipated Gratitude

In other words, you ought to thank God in advance for giving you the victory. Verse 21 gives a fascinating twist to the story. The Bible says that after he consulted the people, Jehoshaphat appointed the choir to march in front of the army, singing and thanking God for His faithfulness before they even got to the battle field!

And the rest of the story? The three enemy armies that were coming against Jehoshaphat and the Israelites ended up getting confused and killing each other. All that God's people had to do was go and pick up the plunder from the sea of bodies lying on the battlefield.

Why did God give them the victory in this way? He did it as an object lesson to teach them, and us today, to praise Him in faith before the victory even takes place.

A boy named James was not a believer. In fact, he was anti-Christian. One day, his mother bought him a Bible, laid it on his desk and said, "Here, son, is your new Bible."

James replied, "What's that for?"

His mother answered, "You don't know it yet, but you're about to become a Christian."

James replied, "No I'm not. I'm going to play football and go to hell."

His mother stood up in church that night and said, "My son is about to become a Christian. He doesn't know it yet, but I'm thanking God in advance."

James's friends began to walk up to him on the street and say, "I heard you became a Christian."

"No, it's just my crazy mother!" He said, "I'm going to play football and go to hell."

But his mother even told her pastor, "I want you to save twenty minutes on Saturday night for my son to give his testimony."

The Friday night before that Saturday, James was playing football when he suddenly felt the presence of God right there on the playing field. He got down on his knees and prayed right in front of everybody: "God, I really need you in my life. If you can make a difference, come in and change me. Save me, whatever it takes. Make me born again."

James ran off the field in his uniform, down the street, and up the stairs into his house. He hugged his mother and said, "Mom, I just became a Christian."

She said, "Of course you did, Hon…I've been telling you that for 3 weeks!"

That is a true story of thanking God in advance. There is power in thankfulness and in having an attitude of gratitude in faith before God.

Today, would you be willing to pray, "Lord, I know I have problems, but I thank you in advance because there is no situation that you can't take care of." A mark of true faith is thanking God in advance.

I recently read about a missionary named Reese House. While in England, God called him to go to Africa, but he first had to find money for train tickets to London and then money for passage to Africa.

One day, God asked, "What would you do if you had the money?" Reese said, "I'd go to London and then get on a ship to Africa."

God asked, "Am I the source of all your needs?"

"Yes."

"Then go."

So Reese and his wife announced to their church, "We're heading to Africa." They only had enough money to get about 50 miles down the road, but they bought train tickets anyway and went as far as they could. Fifty miles later, they found themselves sitting in the train station, feeling foolish.

But God spoke to Reese again. "If you had the money, what would you do?"

"I'd buy a ticket."

God said, "Get in line." He got in line behind about 18 people and stood there. As the line kept getting smaller, Reese kept thinking, "Boy, am I going to look dumb when I get up to that ticket desk!"

When there were only two people ahead of him, Reese said, "Lord! I look stupid here!"

And just then, the man in front of Reese turned around and said, "I've changed my mind. I'm not going. Here! You can have my money."

Would it surprise you to hear that it was enough money to get Reese to Africa?

God's timing is perfect. It always is and it always will be! So the next time you feel discouraged about a problem, don't give up – look up! When you put your hand into the hand of God, you will reach the destiny God has for you. Surrender your problem to your great Provider, and watch Him work a miracle in your life!

# CHAPTER NINE

# Keeping Your Head Above Water

*How to Handle Stress*

Life is full of stress and we all know what it means to have one of those "bad days." I received this e-mail that gave me a good laugh and I would like to share it with you. The title of the e-mail was: "You know you're having a bad day when..."

...You have to hitchhike to the bank to make your car payment.

...The moths in your money belt starve to death.

...People send your wife sympathy cards on your anniversary.

...You wife starts charging you rent.

...The plumber floats by on a kitchen table.

...Your new heart pacemaker has only a 30 day guarantee.

...The pest exterminator crawls under your house and is never seen again.

...People give you a senior citizen discount and you're only 37.

...Your horn gets stuck on the highway behind 32 Hell's Angels motorcyclists.

...Your birthday cake collapses from the weigh of the candles.

...It costs more to fill up your car than it did to buy it.

And this is my favorite: You know you're having a bad day when you wake up in the morning and discover that your waterbed broke. Then you remember that you don't have a waterbed!

Is it not true that too often in life we find ourselves burning the candle at both ends? Occasionally, we all feel like the guy in the cartoon who said, "I try to take just one day at a time but lately several days have attacked me at once." One thing is certain; life is not stress-free.

A businessman wrote this poem based on Psalm 23: "The clock is my dictator, I shall not rest, it makes me to lie down only when exhausted, it leads me to deep depression, it hounds my soul, it leads me in circles of frenzy for activity sake, even though I run frantically from task to task, I will never get it all done, for my ideal is with me, deadlines and my need for approval they drive me, they demand performance from me beyond the limits of my schedule, they anoint my head with migraines; my in-basket overflows, surely fatigue and time limits shall follow me all the days of my life and I will dwell in the bonds of frustration forever." Does that sound like you?

In another storm experience the disciples faced, Jesus said to them, *"It is I, be not afraid"* (John 6:20). In the Greek, He literally is saying, "Be not afraid, I AM." That title, "I AM," is the most sacred name for deity. Jesus was reminding them that He was in existence long before that sea was even a vapor. "I AM" is the eternal proclamation of eternal presence. There was never a time when Jesus was not and there will never be a time when He will not be. When you are in a storm, just remember that Jesus is the "I AM."

Throughout the gospels, Christ has used that title in a number of ways. He said, *"I AM the way, the truth and the life"* (John 14:6). Are you hungry? Jesus said, "I am the bread of life." I AM is an unfinished sentence—you fill in the blank. What need do you have in your life? Jesus is the "I AM" to you. He is not the "I WAS." You cannot live in the failures and disappointments of the past. When you're living in the future, it's hard because He is not the great "I WILL BE." God only gives enough grace to make it through today. Tomorrow is another day and He will meet you there with a new measure of His strength. What we need to do is simply focus on today.

My grandmother kept a sign in her living room that I have thought about ever since I was a small child. I read, "Ain't nothing going to come up today that me and the Lord, together, can't handle."

I have discovered that the cousin to stress is oftentimes worry. Worry pulls tomorrow's clouds over today's sunshine. When you are stressed to the hilt, you will oftentimes find yourself worried to the max! But why do we worry? Worry simply means that there is something over which you cannot have your own way. And most Christians have earned a Ph.D. in worry! It pursues every class of people and every age group as well. In reality, worry is a personal irritation with God because something is going on in your life, or you fear that something may happen in the future, that He has permitted and you cannot control. As a matter of fact, worry is a mild form of atheism. You are not trusting that God is going to take care of you and you are refusing to relenquish your life to Him.

Let me give you a thought that will change your life if you really let it sink in: *God is willing to assume full responsibility for the life that is totally yielded to Him.* Whenever I am tempted to feel full of self-pity because of my inadequacy or insufficiency, I simply reflect on one of my favorite miracles in John's gospel—the feeding of the five thousand. Next to the Lord Jesus, the hero in that story is the little boy who willingly gave up his lunch to help others.

In order to feel the full effect of this parable, you need to know that even though he may have had five barley loaves and two fish, his lunch was barely sufficient to feed himself. Typically, when we think of a loaf of bread, we think about the loaves that we would buy in the grocery store. This boy had barley loaves, the bread of poor people. They were like hard, flat, brittle wafers about the size of a small pancake.

The word for "fish" that John uses is not the word for some big catch of trout. It refers to a little pickled fish which was similar in size to a sardine. This was not a big salmon or a large sea bass; this was just a tiny little minnow. Interestingly, this boy gave up to Jesus what he had even though it was small and insufficient. There is an awesome principle to learn here: Anything that you are willing to *transfer* to Jesus can be *transformed* by Jesus. All that the little boy had became valuable in the hands Christ because he simply made it available.

An old gospel song has a lyric that says: *"If just a cup of water is all that is in your hand; then just a cup of water is all that I demand."* Submit yourself and your stress into the hands of Jesus and allow Him to bless you and multiply your efforts in a way that you never could on your own.

God wants the pressure that is on you to turn your focus to Jesus. Some saltwater fish are able to survive at five thousand feet below sea level. If you tried to submerge yourself to that great depth, the pressure, which is several thousand pounds per square inch, would kill you instantly. So, it's amazing that fish are able to survive and thrive at that depth. What's even more interesting is that these fish don't have to build thick skins in order to make it. They compensate for the outside pressure through equal and opposite pressure inside of themselves. Likewise, we Christians, when the pressure is on, don't have to be hard and thick-skinned to handle the demands of life. We simply have to appropriate God's power within to equal the pressure that is without.

So how can you face the problems in life that cause you stress? I believe that the first work that God wants to do in a believer's life is to change their perspectives, not their problems. In the South, when cotton was "king," the boll weevil crossed over from Mexico to the United States and destroyed the cotton plants. Farmers were forced to grow a variety of crops, such as soybeans and peanuts. They learned to use their land to raise cattle, hogs, and chickens as well. As a result, many farmers became more prosperous than in the days when the only crop grown was cotton.

The people in Enterprise, Alabama, for example, turned from a single-crop system to diversified farming and became wealthier. They were so grateful for what had occurred that they erected a monument to the boll weevil. The inscription on the monument reads: "In profound appreciation of the boll weevil and what it has done to herald prosperity." What looked like a disaster was opportunity wearing a mask. God blessed the bugs.

Some of you who are reading this book are going through a crisis or a stressful time in your life right now. I have a good word from heaven for you—if all you can see is boll weevils, don't worry! God is at work. Proverbs 3:5-6 says, *"Trust in the Lord with all your heart and lean not on your own understanding. In all your ways acknowledge Him and He will direct your paths."* He's leading you to an opportunity that's bigger than anything you've ever dreamed possible.

Ask God to change your attitude about the stress and problems that you are facing right now. What may seem like a source of stress today may be the solution to tomorrow's problem. Dolly Parton summed it all up with these words, "The way I see it, if you want the rainbow you gotta put up with the rain."

John Maxwell says that there is a world of difference between a person who has a big problem and a person who makes a problem big. A lot of Christians who whine over how stressful their life is aren't necessarily the ones who have the most problems. They are the ones who are problem conscious and find their difficulties stressful. Their "problems" are not their real problem. The problem is that they react wrongly to "problems" and therefore make their "problems" the real problem. What really counts is not what happens *to me* but what happens *in me*. The size of the person is more important than the size of the problem. Problems look larger or smaller according to whether the person is large or small.

Richard Sloma says never try to solve the difficulties that cause you stress all at once—make them line up for you one-by-one. Whether you face three problems, thirty, or three hundred, "make them stand in single file so you face only one at a time."

My wife, Carrie, has kept a poem on her desk that I believe speaks volumes on how to experience a victorious life in the midst of the calamity of daily living. It's a poem by Ralph Cushman entitled, "I Met God in the Morning":

I met God in the morning
When my day was at its best,
And His presence came like sunrise
Like a glory in my breast.
All day long His presence lingered,
All day long He stayed with me,
And we sailed in perfect calmness
O'er every troubled sea.

Other ships were blown and battered,
Other ships were sore distressed
But the winds that seemed to drive them
Brought to us both peace and rest.

Then I thought of other mornings,
With a keen remorse of mind,
When I too, had loosed the moorings
With the Presence left behind.

So I think I know the secret
Learned from many a troubled way;
You must seek Him in the morning
If you want Him through the day.

CHAPTER TEN

# Living Above "See" Level

*Walking By Faith, Not By Sight*

We've often heard that little motto: "What you see is what you get." That's the world's way of saying what is real are those things you can see, touch, taste, smell, and hear. In other words, reality is what we can handle with our five senses. We know there is another real world out there and that is the unseen world.

Growing up in Florida, I have experienced my fair share of hurricanes. They are by far the most destructive form of nature known to man. I can recall on one occasion, a category one hurricane was projected to hit our area. Since this was a storm that did not pack as much power as some of the other hurricanes that have hit South Florida, my family decided not to evacuate but to ride the storm out at home. It was certainly an experience, to say the least. All of our windows were boarded up and we slept in the hallways of our home. We were unable to see the force of the winds and rain in person, but we could certainly hear what was going on outside!

I find it interesting that when hurricanes first make landfall, it seems as if all hell breaks loose. Then, the eye of the storm passes over you and it is eerily calm, peaceful and still. You look straight up into clear blue skies, knowing that this moment of silence is only temporary, that the other half of the storm is barreling toward you.

I think back to those hurricane experiences whenever I face storms of a different nature. I simply look into the face of God and ask that He would hold me in the very center of His hand. When you reach that position, then and only then, are you able to look up clearly into the face of God. In that position with our Lord, you will experience the complete "peace that surpasses all understanding" and that "joy unspeakable" no matter what your difficulty. If, however, you wander off-center from God during your storm, you will likely experience all the fury that storm has to offer. The key is in being in a right relationship with God twenty-four hours a day, seven days a week.

In the Bible, there are two different kinds of storms. Certainly, there are "correcting" storms that we face when we are living in rebellion against God. Jonah is a prime example. God had told him to go to Ninevah and to proclaim to them a message of repentance. If you know the story, you'll remember that Jonah disobeyed and ended up getting a full three nights stay on a "foam blubber mattress" (the belly of a whale). There are correcting storms, but as we have seen already, there are also "perfecting' storms. As I mentioned earlier, the disciples were in a storm not because they were out of the will of God but because they were in the will of God.

We need to learn to live above "see" level. In other words, we need to peer through the lens of faith to see the bigger picture. One of the greatest blessings that God wants to bestow upon your life during this time is the gift of perspective. He wants you to be able to view your problems through His eyes. Remember that "Faith is like film—it is only developed in the dark." It is only in the darkroom of God's providence that the undeveloped negatives of your life are turned into the portraits of His providence.

Back when our cameras used to use 35 mm film, we would all take pictures and send them to the developer. The pictures are originally on the negatives, which aren't really great to look at. The pictures are small and not easy to see. So in order to get pictures that you can see, the developers have to take the negatives to the darkroom where they can be developed in secret. When the pictures come back to you, they are larger and now in color. The final product looks nothing like the original image on the negative. In order to the get the final product, however, the negatives have to be taken to a dark room where they are worked over by the man in the photo lab.

We can't always see what God is doing. It may look like all we are getting is one negative after another. However, there is good news. God is working on the negatives in a dark room, in secret where we can't see. When it is the right time, He will bring them back in living color. We will see that He was up to something and working something out that we didn't know about. He has a purpose for every trial that you face. He has a reason for your development in your trial.

When the Israelites were about to head into the Promised Land, twelve spies were sent into Canaan to scope out the territory. Ten out of those twelve spies said, "There's no way that we can take this land! There are demon-possessed giants out there and we are like grasshoppers in our own sight!" Two of those spies saw things from a different perspective.

In Numbers 14, the two spies said that those same giants "were bread for us." That's an interesting comparison. You eat bread for strength. You grow from bread. Those very things that seem like tremendous obstacles, those things that look like major problems, are your food. It is when you feed on these problems, in the right way, that you grow. God isn't looking for softees as disciples. His goal is not to make us wimps but warriors. You are growing by his plan and it is in the storm that you become more and more like Jesus.

When God waits to intervene on your behalf, His timing is always strategic and deliberate. Isaiah 30:18 says, *"And therefore will the Lord wait that He may be gracious unto you."* God is waiting upon you to wait upon Him. Have you ever thought about the deliberate delays of the Lord? The gospels say that when Jesus found out that Lazarus had died, he waited two days before he did anything. By the time Jesus got to where the body of Lazarus was laid in his graveclothes, four days had passed. Jesus had a plan there and He still chose to raise Lazarus from the dead. Suppose Jesus had come right away and healed Lazarus. Some skeptic may have said, "Well, the man might have gotten better anyway." No friend, God had a plan. His plan didn't make sense to Mary and Martha, and His plans may not always make sense to us, but it does make sense to Jesus! So many times, we try to pick God's blessings before they're ripe. God is working in your life to develop patience. He is never in a hurry and He is never late.

*One by one God took them from me*
*All the things I valued most*
*Till I was empty handed*
*Every glittering toy was lost.*
*And I walked earth's highways*
*Grieving in my rags and poverty*
*Until I heard His voice inviting*
*"Lift those empty hands to me."*

*And I turned my hands toward heaven*
*And He filled them with a store*
*Of His own transcendent riches*

*Till they could contain no more.*

*And at last I comprehended*

*With my mind stupid and dull,*

*That God could not pour His riches*

*Into hands already full.*

In 2 Timothy 4:18, Paul makes a bold statement. He said, *"The Lord will rescue me from every evil deed, and will bring me safely to His heavenly kingdom..."* There is a phrase in that verse that really grabbed my attention. Paul said that God would rescue Him from *"every evil deed."* Either that statement is true or not. And since it is in the Word of God, then that means that we can draw a conclusion. If you are a Christian, God will rescue you from every evil deed.

It gets a little confusing, though, when you think about what happened to the man who wrote that verse, the Apostle Paul. He never made it out of the dark dungeon in which he was writing this epistle. Even worse, Paul eventually was beheaded. So how is it that he could have written under the inspiration of God, *"The Lord will rescue me from every evil deed"*? The word "rescue" or "deliver" literally means, "to be taken from the presence of." There are two ways in which you can be rescued: you can have the danger taken away from you or you can be taken away from the danger.

Perhaps you know that you are a Christian and you have just been diagnosed with cancer. The doctors have told you that you are suffering from a terminal illness. Your prognosis is that you are not going to recover. We all know that God can heal you. Our God is the Great Physician and all healing ultimately comes from the hand of God. What you may or may not realize is that God can heal you in one of two ways. Either God can heal you *temporarily* or God can heal you *permanently*. So what is the difference? God will sometimes choose to heal one of His children temporarily. In other words, He takes the disease away from you. Other times, God will say, "I'm going to do something better than that. I will heal you permanently." In this case, he takes you away from the disease. Sometimes God heals physically and other times God heals eternally.

Not long ago, I preached the funeral for my own grandmother. She had been struggling with her health in a nursing home for a long time. God did not take the disease away from my grandmother; God took my grandmother away from that disease.

I don't know what Granny Park is doing in heaven today but I will tell you this: she's not struggling with her health ailments, she's not paying taxes, and she's not having to deal with the every day cares and struggles of this world.

David said in that famous Psalm, 23:4, "*Yea though I walk through the valley of the shadow of death, I will fear no evil.*" Notice that David calls death a "shadow." A shadow, although it may be intimidating, cannot harm you. The shadow of a sword or of a snake cannot hurt you. Only two things are necessary in order to make a shadow: a light and a substance. Jesus, the light of the world, has taken dominion over the substance of death. Whenever I die, I am going to pass through a harmless shadow that cannot hurt me. It is only a transport from this veil of tears into the presence of His glory. I am more than a conqueror because Christ has defeated the enemy of the grave.

So God will rescue you from "every evil deed." Faith is not receiving from God what you want; Faith is accepting from God what He gives. If you go through something in your life and God does not rescue you from it, it wasn't an evil deed. The only thing that is evil for your life is anything that lies outside of the will of God for your life. Nothing else!

When you feel like you are going through a time of darkness, you need to learn how to "glow in the dark." When I was a little kid, I used to be fascinated with those Glow-in-the-dark products. I had a glow-in-the-dark yo-yo, a glow-in-the-dark ball, and I even had glow-in-the-dark pajamas (it made it easier for my parents to find me at night).

It's amazing how these glow-in-the-dark toys actually work. All of these products contain a chemical substance known as phosphor. Phosphor is simply a substance that radiates visible light. In order to make objects glow, they first have to be "charged" or "energized" by a light source. You expose them to the light and then, when the room gets dark, they let out a radiant glow.

The Bible says, *"In God's presence there is fullness of joy; at your right hand are pleasures forevermore."* So how can you keep your joy in the darkness? You have to allow yourself to be exposed to the light of God's presence. When you "charge" and "energize" your spirit by fellowshiping with Him, it will be His joy that radiates and emanates out of you during your darkest hour. C.S. Lewis said, "God whispers to us in our pleasures, speaks in our conscience, but shouts in our pains; it is His megaphone to rouse a deaf world." Psalm 16:7-9, *"I will bless the Lord who counsels me, he gives me wisdom in the night. He tells me what to do. I am always thinking of the Lord; and because he is so near, I never need to stumble or to fall. Heart body and soul are filled with joy."* (TLB)

There was a boy who was looking at the reflection of the moon glistening in a pond. A friend of his threw a stone into the pond and the water began to ripple. The boy said, "What happened to the moon?" The stone thrown into the pond so rippled the water that he could no longer see the reflection of the moon and it looked like the moon was gone.

His older friend said, "When you can't see the moon in the pond, stop looking at the pond and look up to the moon because the moon hasn't gone anywhere." When you cannot find God in your circumstances, stop delving into your circumstances and look up to – the Father of Lights – because Jehovah Jireh, your Provider hasn't gone anywhere.

During the New York City blackout of 2003, the people of New York didn't know what to do. Everything in the city was totally blacked out. For the first time, this city of lights was pitch black dark. People began to go out into the streets so that they could at least see through the light of the full moon.

One reporter said that he overheard one little girl who apparently was born and lived in New York City all her little life. She was on her Daddy's shoulders and all of a sudden she looked up into the sky and she exclaimed, "Daddy! What are those! There are hundreds of them!"

Because she had lived in New York City all her life, the brightness of the city lights would not permit you to see the stars. And now, with all of the distractions from this world down here removed; she was able to get a glimpse of another world up there!

Sometimes God has to allow us to go through a "blackout" in order for us to look up to Him and to see His face more clearly.

A wise man once said that we should never doubt in the dark what God has shown us in the light. You may not understand everything that is happening to you, but your relationship with God is more important than a list of reasons. It may be that we do not know the *why* in order that we may know the *who*. I believe that even if the Lord were to give us all the reasons for why He does what He does, many of us still wouldn't understand it all or be satisfied. So God gives us something much better than reasons and explanations…He gives us Himself.

I heard the story of a little girl whose mother passed away. Her first night apart from her mother was very difficult. She felt alone in the darkness of her bedroom and left it to sleep with her father. They tried to get some sleep, but the little girl said, "Daddy, it's so dark. Have you ever seen it so dark?"

The father said, "No, darling, I have never seen it this dark."

Then the little girl, who could not even see her father's face in the dark, asked him, "Daddy, is your face toward me?"

"Yes, darling, my face is toward you."

"Daddy, you love me through the dark, don't you?"

"Yes, sweetheart, Daddy loves you through the dark."

And with that assurance, the little girl drifted off to sleep.

Later on that night, the father slipped out of bed, fell on his knees, and prayed, "Heavenly Father, it is so dark. I don't think I have ever felt it this dark before. Lord Jesus, is your face toward me?"

He sensed in his spirit an answer from heaven that said, "Yes, my child, my face is toward you."

"Heavenly Father, You love me through the dark, don't You?"

"Yes, My child, I love you through the darkest night."

And with that assurance, the father joined his precious daughter in some much needed sleep.

If the lights have gone out and you feel as if you are in the dark, learn to live above see level. Ask God to help you learn the lessons that can only be learned in darkness. And thank Him that He loves you through the dark and will one day flood you with His light once again.

# CHAPTER ELEVEN

# Coming Safely to the Other Side

*In the End, You Will Win!*

So what is the key to passing through your storm successfully? How is it that you can come safely to the other side? In essence, what you must do is hang on to the Lord Jesus Christ and don't let go. I can remember as a little boy, whenever I would get around a large crowd of people and was afraid that I would be lost, I would look to find my father's hand and I would hold on tight and not let go! When the storms rage, seek your heavenly Father, take hold of His divine hand, and He will never let you go. He will surround you with the peace that passes all understanding and envelope you with His unending grace.

Horratio Spafford was a man that knew what it meant to encounter storms in his life. He was a very successful businessman but during the great Chicago fire that took place during the 1800's, he lost all his possessions and his thriving business. In an effort to start a new life, he wanted to move his family to Jerusalem where he could serve the Lord in ministry. In 1873, he sent his wife and four children on a ship to cross the Atlantic while he made the final preparations back in America to move. During the ship's voyage across the ocean, the vessel sank and his four children perished. Anna, his wife, once she was rescued sent a telegram back to Horratio with the dreadful words, "Saved Alone."

A few weeks later, Spafford set sail aboard a ship to France to be reunited with His wife. When the ship was about halfway across the Atlantic, the captain called him up to the bridge and showed him the location where his four children had died. That night, as Horratio

Spafford looked over that barren sea where the tragedy occurred, he penned the words to a hymn that Christians have sung for many years:

*"When peace like a river attendeth my way;*
*When sorrows like sea billows roll;*
*Whatever my lot, Thou hast taught me to say,*
*It is well, it is well, with my soul."*

I can imagine that Spafford experienced the presence of God, a divine peace and comfort, like never before during the worst storm that he would ever face in his life. The storm battered him emotionally, mentally, possibly even spiritually, but Horratio Spafford emerged victorious in the Lord. He overcame a deep agony in his spirit from his loss to stand with a deep joy in his soul from his gain. As I sing the hymn Spafford wrote, I know that God rewarded him for turning over the controls of his storm-tossed life and allowing God to drive.

There are many rewards for overcoming our stormy trials. There is an *external reward* in knowing that tomorrow is another day. God can and will lead you from trouble to triumph but it must come in His divine timing. Eventually, there will be a change of circumstances. There is also an *internal reward.* Just as Horratio Spafford experienced a divine peace and comfort, we too can experience this increase in our faith. There are some things about the Lord that we can only learn through trials. The greatest reward we can receive, however, is our *eternal reward.* James 1:12 says, *"Blessed is a man who perseveres under trial; for once he has been approved, he will receive the crown of life, which the Lord has promised to those who love Him."*

How long will your storm last? Only God knows. But I do know this: if you draw closer to Christ in the midst of your crisis, you will see a reward greater than anything you could have thought of on your own.

Back when my wife, Carrie, and I were dating, I took her to a local fair we had in Virginia. I have always loved going to fairs and we enjoyed all of the rides and festivities. One of the last rides that we rode was called, "The Hurricane." It was one of those rides that rigorously spun you around and around until you almost lost your lunch! I have to admit that I had an ulterior motive for getting on that ride. I sat on the outer edge of the ride so that, the faster it went, the closer that Carrie would be to my side! I think that is also what our Heavenly Father has in mind. He wants us to draw close to His side when trouble throws us in every direction.

It is important for believers to remember that no matter what comes our way, God is in control of the situation; God is still going to take care of us. The story has been told of a believer, Frederick Nolan, who was fleeing from his enemies during a time of persecution in North Africa. Nolan was fleeing on foot from the very ones who sought to end his life. He ran until he could not go any further and found a small cave to hind inside. He just knew that these enemies who were hot on his trail would inevitably find him. In the back of the cave, he collapsed and looked towards the light at the opening – fearing the worst and waiting for his demise. While he sat there, he said his final prayers to God and he watched as a small spider weaved a web across the mouth of that cave until eventually the web covered most of the opening. When those pursuers arrived in that area, they wondered if Nolan could have been hiding inside, but on seeing the unbroken and unmangled piece of art, they thought it would have been impossible for him to have entered that cave without first dismantling the web. And so they went on.

Having escaped, Nolan went on to write about his experience and he wrote: "Where God is, a spider's web is like a wall; where God is not, a wall is like a spider's web." There is no need to wonder how God will take care of you; just be assured that He will.

In Max Lucado's book, *When Christ Comes,* he shares a touching real-life story. In 1989, the nation of Armenia was devastated with the worst earthquake that it had ever experienced in its history. One reporter did a documentary on a father and his six year old son, Arman. This father and son had no one else in their family; it was just the two of them. The mother had passed away many years earlier and, because of that experience, the dad and the boy developed an extremely close bond. The father had a routine that he did every day with his son. He would walk his little boy to school every morning and, before saying goodbye, he would give him a big hug and say, "Arman, I love you! And I want you to remember that I will never leave you and that I will always be there for you!"

It seemed like an ordinary weekday morning. The father had just finished taking his son to school before heading off to work. Shortly thereafter, the devastating earthquake hit. Experts say that nearly 30,000 people died instantly in this terrible disaster.

Immediately after the earthquake had subsided, the dad left his work and ran to the school to see if his son was ok. He could not have prepared his heart for what he was about to see. As soon as he arrived, his heart was filled with the most dreadful and agonizing heartache one could ever imagine. What used to be his son's elementary school was now a mountainous pile of rock and rubble on the ground. Other parents were already there, crying and mourning over the apparent loss of their children.

The man rushed over to the other parents and pleaded with them to him him find their children but they were too distraught to help. So, he singlehandedly climbed the mountain of debris to begin the grueling process of digging through the rubble in order to find his son. For thirty-six grueling hours, he worked non-stop. Witnesses said that his hands were extremely bloody and blistered from the painstaking work of trying to lift and pull away those heavy boulders of concrete. As he lifted away several large bricks that were covering a small opening, he began to hear a faint but familiar voice.

"Dad! Dad! Is that you, Dad?"

The father yelled, "Arman!!! Is that you, son?"

"Yes Dad, it's me! I'm ok. The rest of my class is here under this table with me. We are all ok. I knew that you would come for me, Dad!"

You could imagine the reunion that father and son must have had as he reached down into that crevice and pulled out his son and the rest of the little boys and girls in that class. As they were walking back home, they were each filled with relief and joy knowing that the other was safe and sound. But then a thought occurred to the father. He stopped his son and knelt down to where he could look at him in the face and said, "Arman, how in the world did you know it was me? You couldn't see me. I couldn't see you. What made you think that it was your daddy that was pulling away the debris trying to rescue you?

The little boy looked up at his father with those big brown eyes and said, "Because, Daddy, you made me a promise. You told me that you would always be there for me and that you would never leave me!"

Friend, that is exactly the promise that you have in the Lord Jesus Christ. He, Himself, has said, *"I will never leave you nor forsake you."* In the midst of your storm, Christ offers to you His strength, His presence, and His supply. God has not promised you smooth sailing but He has promised you a safe landing. You will never face difficulty by yourself. Together, with your Lord, you can survive the storm.

CHAPTER TWELVE

# Is Jesus In Your Boat?

*You Can Be Sure!*

I would not want to close this book without first telling you
how you can experience an abundant life here on earth and an eternal
life with God in heaven. I simply want to ask you to reflect on two
questions that I believe will be the most important questions you need
to answer in this life.

**First, are you 100% sure that if you were to die today you would
go to heaven?**

You may be thinking, "Well, I would probably have to say that
I am 50% sure or maybe even 90%. But the Word of God tells us in I
John 5:13, "*These things I have written to you who believe in the name of the Son
of God so that you might know that you have eternal life.*" God doesn't want
you to have a "hope-so" salvation but a "know-so" salvation. God
does not want you to be a doubting Christian, He wants you to be a
shouting Christian! You can't tell me that you are content with a "90%
assurance" when your eternal destiny weighs in the balance! You need
to be completely sure of it and God's Word teaches that you can be.
Dwight L. Moody once said, "I have never met anybody who was any
good to the service of Christ who first of all did not have assurance of
his or her salvation.

**Secondly, if you were to meet Christ face to face and He were to ask you "Why should I let you into heaven?" what do you think you would say?**

Basically, there are three answers that people will give in response to this question.

**The Answer of Behavior.** You might say, "Well I'm a good person. I try to live a moral life." If you have this kind of mindset, you think that if the good you have done outweighs the bad then someday when you get to heaven, if the scales tip in your favor, God will let you in. Friend, this is one of the greatest lies that Satan feeds to people. If you could be a good, moral person and still make it into heaven, Jesus would not have had to die for your sins. Ephesians 2:8-9 says, *"For by grace you have been saved through faith; and that not of yourselves, it is the gift of God; not as a result of works, so that no one may boast."*

**The Answer of Birth:** How many times have you heard people say, "I've been a Christian ALL my life"? If you are this person, as sincere as you might be, you have missed what it means to truly be a Christian. Christianity is not something you are humanly born into. Being born into a Christian home doesn't make you a Christian anymore than being born in a hospital makes you a doctor!

**The Answer of Belief.** There is only one door to heaven. It is not the back door of behavior; it is not the side door of birth; it is the front door of belief. In John 14:6, *"Jesus answered, I am the way and the truth and* *the life, no man cometh unto the Father but by me!"* The only answer to man's problem, to your problem, is to believe in the Lord Jesus Christ.

Most people make the mistake of thinking that church is all about religion. God hates man's religion. What separates Christianity from Islam, Buddhism, Hinduism and all other world beliefs is that they all are attempts to reach upward to God. Christianity is the only religion that has God reaching down to man. There is a big difference between man's religion and the gospel of Jesus Christ.

- Religion says, "Try," but the gospel says, "trust."

- Religion says, "Pay me what you owe." The gospel says, "I'll pay what you owe."

- Religion says, "Live for God." The gospel says, "Live through God."

- Religion says, "Obey the law," but the gospel says, "Obey the Lord."

- Religion says "Do," but the gospel says, "Done."

- Religion says, "Attain righteousness." The gospel says, "Accept righteousness."

- Religion says, "My way is the right way." The gospel says, "God's way is the only way."

- Religion says "Salvation is in a formula." The gospel says, "Salvation is by faith."

- Religion says "Believe something," but the gospel says, "Receive someone!"

You don't need dead rituals or dry religion. What you need is a Divine Redeemer, and His name is Jesus Christ!

Jesus said in John 10:10, *"I have come that you might have life and have it more abundantly."* The best way that I know to explain to you how you can have this kind of relationship with God is by using the acronym L.I.F.E.

## Love

God made man to love Him forever. The Bible says in John 3:16, *"For God so loved the world that He gave His one and only son, so that whosoever should believe in Him, would not perish but have eternal life."* God created you to live in a relationship with Him. God wants to offer you hope, peace, and a purpose for why you are here on this earth. The best news I could ever tell you is that God has a wonderful plan for your life. He loves you and desires for you to be in a right relationship with Him. Romans 5:8 says, *"But God demonstrates His own love toward us in that while we were yet sinners, Christ died for us."* God loves you so much that He would send His Son to die for you. Even if you were the only person on the face of this earth, Jesus Christ still would have died for you. You are special to Him.

But if God loves you and desires a relationship with you, then why is it that you feel so isolated from Him? That brings me to the next point...

## Isolation

Sin, the wrong things that you and I have done, is what isolates us from God. It builds a wall that separates humanity from God. Sin is rebellion against God and keeps us from experiencing eternal life in heaven and abundant life on earth.

Here are two basic facts about sin:

All of us have sinned. The Bible says in Romans 3:23, *"For all have sinned and fall short of the glory of God."* There is not a single person reading this book who has lived a perfect life, and that is why we need a perfect Savior.

Sin is the cause of physical and spiritual death. Romans 6:23 says, *"For the wages of sin is death."* If you were to take all the nuclear weapons in the world, strap them to your body and detonate them, it would vaporize your body in a nanosecond, but it wouldn't take away the sin that is in your soul. Only the blood of Jesus Christ can blow sin out of a man's heart. Only the blood of Jesus Christ can cleanse us and make us pure and make us clean.

I would be cruel if I did not warn you that hell is a reality. God has never sent a single person to hell. People send themselves to hell by not accepting His free gift of eternal life.

So how can you get past this isolation and experience a "relationship with Jesus Christ." God wants to offer you His forgiveness...

**Forgiveness**

Forgiveness is the only solution to the isolation problem.

The only way that our relationship can be restored with God is for our sins to be forgiven. Jesus Christ died on the cross for that very purpose. I Peter 3:18 says, *"Jesus died for all sins once for everyone...to bring you to God.*" His death made it possible to be forgiven but you have to ask for it.

## Eternal Life

Eternal life and a one-on-one relationship with God can be a reality for you now and forever. John 1:12 says, *"Yet to all who have received Him* (Jesus) *to those who have believed in His name, He gave the right to become children of God."*

The ability to have the life that you've always dreamed about is right within your grasp. Do you want that life today – an abundant life on earth and eternal life in heaven? It's as easy as A.B.C.

**A**dmit you are a sinner and that you are willing to make a 180 degree turn from your sin. That's what it means to repent. Acts 3:19 says, "Repent, then, and turn to God, so that your sins may be wiped out."

**B**elieve that Jesus died for your sins and rose again from the dead.

**C**onfess verbally and publicly your belief in Jesus Christ. *"That if you confess with your mouth 'Jesus is Lord,' and believe in your heart that God raised Him from the dead, you will be saved."* (Romans 10:9)10

Life's greatest discovery is that you can go to heaven by faith in the Lord Jesus Christ. You don't have to pay for your sins — Jesus has already paid. You don't have to die in your sins —Jesus has already died. You don't have to do something for God; you just have to accept what God has done for you.    Augustine said, "God loves you as if there were nobody else left to love." He is willing to receive and accept you just as you are if you will receive and accept Him. God wants to save you for more than just eternity. He wants to save you so that He can take up residence in your life.

If you would like to receive Jesus Christ into your life as your Savior and Lord, I would like to suggest a prayer that you can pray to become a Christian and a lifelong follower of Christ.   Remember, it's not the words that you pray that are important, it is the attitude of your heart.   If you are willing to surrender yourself to the Lord Jesus Christ, get on your knees before God and pray something like this:

*"Dear God, I know that I am a sinner and that I cannot save myself. Please come into my life, take control of my life, and be my Lord and Savior. I turn away from my old way of living and I want to live for you. I receive and accept your free gift of eternal life by faith in the Lord Jesus Christ. Thank you for answering my prayer and giving me the assurance of my salvation. In Jesus' name, Amen.*

Did you pray that prayer and mean it with all your heart? If so, the Bible teaches that, just now, you became a child of God. You were "born-again" as the Bible says.   I want to encourage you to let our ministry know by contacting us with the information below. We will send you some free resources that will help you get started in your newfound walk with Jesus Christ.    May God richly bless you as you begin your journey as a lifelong follower of Jesus Christ!

ATTN: Office of the Senior Pastor

Wayside Baptist Church

7701 SW 98th Street

Miami, Florida 33156

(305) 595-6550 (ext. 105)